Twayne's English Authors Series

EDITOR OF THIS VOLUME

Kinley E. Roby

Northeastern University

George Fitzmaurice

TEAS 252

LEFT: Only photograph of George Fitzmaurice in existence, taken in the early 1940s at about age 65.

Courtesy of Professor Howard Slaughter

RIGHT: Daugh House in 1934, the Fitzmaurice ancestral home.

Courtesy of Professor Howard Slaughter

GEORGE FITZMAURICE

By CAROL W. GELDERMAN

University of New Orleans

TWAYNE PUBLISHERS

A DIVISION OF G. K. HALL & CO., BOSTON

Copyright © 1979 by G.K. Hall & Co.

Published in 1979 by Twayne Publishers,
A Division of G. K. Hall & Co.
All Rights Reserved

Printed on permanent/durable acid-free paper and bound in the
United States of America

First Printing

Library of Congress Cataloging in Publication Data
Gelderman, Carol W
George Fitzmaurice.
(Twayne's English authors series; TEAS 252)
Bibliography: p. 155-61
Includes index.
1. Fitzmaurice, George—Criticism and interpretation.
I. Title
PR6011.I9Z68   822'.9'12   78-13027
ISBN 0-8057-6741-X

Contents

About the Author

Carol W. Gelderman joined the English faculty at the University of New Orleans in 1972 and is currently Associate Professor. A native of Michigan, she received her undergraduate education at Manhattanville College and her Master's and Ph.D. degrees from Northwestern University. Having a specialty in modern drama, Professor Gelderman has published articles on current theater in *Prairie Schooner,* in *EIRE–Ireland* and in *Lost Generation Journal,* and has contracted to do a drama anthology for Scott–Foresman.

Preface

George Fitzmaurice is best known for his comedy, *The Country Dressmaker*, produced at the Abbey Theatre in 1907, although he wrote plays for the next fifty years. It is the aim of this critical study of Fitzmaurice not only to make his work better known, but to assess the value of his literary achievement.

The introductory chapter of the book presents basic facts about Fitzmaurice's life and work. Chapter 2 gives background material, namely, a short history of the Abbey Theater and discusses George Fitzmaurice as short-story writer. Chapter 3 considers Fitzmaurice's dramatic work with reference to recurring themes, language, and setting.

Chapter 4 is concerned with Fitzmaurice's dramatic techniques, conventional and experimental. George Fitzmaurice began and ended his career writing realistic plays. In the middle of his career he wrote folk fantasies which, when successful, dramatized the folk imagination of the peasants from his native Kerry (a county in the west of Ireland) in their fusion of peasant superstition and fantasy with everyday farm life. His dramatic techniques in staging his folk vignettes are unique in that he has tried to preserve the folktale as nearly as possible in its distinctive narrative form, and yet mold that form into drama. Chapter 5 provides brief discussion of the lesser plays.

Chapter 6 offers an assessment of Fitzmaurice's dramatic talent in the context of the achievement of his fellow folk playwrights, Synge and Lady Gregory. Chapter 7 disproves the many allegations that Fitzmaurice is unknown today because Yeats, the most powerful of the Abbey directors, deliberately kept Fitzmaurice off the Abbey stage because he was afraid of a potential rival. Chapter 8 provides a summary.

Overall, comment on the literary output of Fitzmaurice is extremely small. In my study of Fitzmaurice I came to a richer understanding of what his fellow folk dramatists, Synge and Lady Gregory were producing, an understanding about which I have written in this book. Moreover, I came to see Fitzmaurice as the most authentic of the Irish folk dramatists. Finally, I have made an attempt to rescue a neglected playwright from an undeserved obscurity.

CAROL GELDERMAN

University of New Orleans

Acknowledgments

I wish gratefully to acknowledge permission from Liam Miller, publisher of the Dolmen Press, to quote from the works of George Fitzmaurice as indicated: *The Plays of George Fitzmaurice: Dramatic Fantasies* edited by Austin Clarke; *The Plays of George Fitzmaurice: Folk Plays* and *The Plays of George Fitzmaurice: Realistic Plays* both edited by Howard K. Slaughter; and *The Crows of Mephistopheles and Other Stories*, edited by Robert Hogan.

I also wish to thank Eoin McKiernan, president of the Irish American Cultural Institute for permission to use, in a somewhat revised form, an essay I published in the institute's quarterly journal *EIRE-Ireland* in the summer of 1973.

Chronology

1877　George Fitzmaurice born January 28 in Bedford House near Listowel, County Kerry, province of Munster, Ireland.

1900　Publishes "Peter Fagan's Veiled Bride," "Maeve's Grand Love," and "The Plight of Lena's Wooers."

1901　Becomes a clerk in Dublin office of Congested Districts Board. Publishes "Peter Praisin" and "The Disappearance of Mrs. Mulreany."

1904　"The Bashfulness of Philip Reilly."

1906　"Cupid and Cornelius."

1907　"The Streel" and "The Crows of Mephistopheles." October 3, *The Country Dressmaker* produced by the Abbey company.

1908　March 10, *The Pie-Dish* opens at the Abbey.

1909　February, *The Pie-Dish* goes on tour to the Gaiety Theatre in Manchester, England.

1913　April 24, *The Magic Glasses* is produced at the Abbey.

1914　*Five Plays*. Joins British army; serves in France.

1917　American edition of *Five Plays*.

1918　Goes to work for Land Commission.

1923　March 8, *'Twixt the Giltinans and the Carmodys* opens at the Abbey.

1924　*The Linnaun Shee.*

1926　*The Green Stone.*

1932　Transfers to Department of Agriculture.

1943　*'Twixt the Giltinans and the Carmodys.*

1945　Austin Clarke's Lyric Theatre produces *The Dandy Dolls* and *The Magic Glasses.*

1948　The Earlsfort Players produce *The Moonlighter* and *The Magic Glasses.* Publishes *There Are Tragedies and Tragedies.*

1949　*One Evening Gleam.* The Green Circle Theatre Club produces *The Magic Glasses.* Austin Clarke's Lyric Theatre stages *The Linnaun Shee.*

1952   St. Mary's College produces *There Are Tragedies and Tragedies.* Liam Miller stages *One Evening Gleam* at the Studio Theatre Club in Dublin.

1954   *The Coming of Ewn Andzale* and *The Terrible Baisht.*

1957   *The Enchanted Land.*

1963   May 12, George Fitzmaurice dies in Dublin.

1966   July, *The Enchanted Land* produced by Howard Slaughter at the Mischler Theatre in Altoona, Pennsylvania.

1967   *The Toothache.*

1969   February, *The Country Dressmaker* produced by University of Akron.

CHAPTER 1

Introduction

I N official histories of the Irish theater, George Fitzmaurice receives brief recognition as the author of a rural comedy called *The Country Dressmaker*. First staged at the Abbey October 3, 1907, nine months after *The Playboy of the Western World* made its spectacular and riotous appearance, it was criticized by Yeats, who thought it would produce another riot.

> I have just come up from Coole for the production of a new play called *The Country Dressmaker*. It is by a new writer called Fitzmaurice. A harsh, strong, ugly comedy. It really gives a much worse view of the people than *The Playboy*. Even I rather dislike it, though I admire its sincerity, and yet it was received with enthusiasm.... Of course, we may not get through tomorrow night, but the row won't be very bad.... We may have had another performance of *The Country Dressmaker* since I wrote, and the success was greater than before.[1]

And four days later Yeats wrote to Florence Farr calling *The Country Dressmaker* "a rough but amusing piece of work which is showing signs of being popular."[2]

As it turned out, the show was a great success. Far from arousing a fresh uproar, it brought back the Dublin public which John Millington Synge has estranged from the theater; and the Abbey, making the most of this change of fortune, suspended its normal repertory and extended the play's run. Maire O'Neill, Sara Allgood, and other Abbey favorites were in the cast, and Fitzmaurice took a curtain call with them each night *The Country Dressmaker* played.

Joseph Holloway, the Dublin architect who achieved a mild local notoriety for having never missed an Abbey opening night from its beginnings in 1899 until his death in the early 1940s wrote: "No troops required, not even a policeman, at the Abbey

13

tonight when George Fitzmaurice's three act comedy of life in North Kerry, entitled *The Country Dressmaker*, was presented for the first time on the stage. Yeats is a false prophet where Irish character is concerned.... A large, fashionable, and most appreciative audience assembled to do the new playwright justice, and give his first staged work an attentive and unprejudiced hearing."[3]

This was the only real success of George Fitzmaurice's career. He was thirty years old at the time, a temporary clerk in the Dublin office of the Congested Districts Board, with little experience of the theater except as an ardent music-hall fan. After *The Country Dressmaker* he wrote an extraordinary one-actor called *The Pie-Dish* which had a disastrous run at the Abbey in the following year. Five years later *The Magic Glasses* was staged, equally unsuccessfully, and ten years after this failure the Abbey put on *'Twixt the Giltinans and the Carmodys*. Apart from periodic revivals of *The Country Dressmaker*, the Abbey ignored Fitzmaurice for the rest of his life.

I *Life*

Fitzmaurice was born on January 28, 1877 near Listowel, County Kerry. The Fitzmaurices were an old family able to trace their roots to the Norman Conquest. In Ireland, especially in County Kerry, the country gentry were a close knit community and seldom married out of their own class—at least before the turn of the century. George's father was a clergyman in the Church of Ireland, and had been a very fine classical scholar at Trinity College. Even so, he married a local girl of peasant stock, a Catholic by the name of Winifred O'Connor, the daughter of one of his tenants, in 1861, when he was thirty-nine and she was nineteen. A mixed marriage was exceedingly unusual at that time.

The couple lived at Bedford House, a large though architecturally undistinguished home, in the township of Listowel in North Kerry. As the younger son of the Big House, the Reverend Fitzmaurice, was not well off. He educated his family of seven girls and five boys at home. Thus George was not able to enter any of the professions undertaken by so many of his relations, among whom were doctors, lawyers, admirals, and engineers. Worse, by this marriage, Parson George lost all social standing for his children among the gentry.

The Fitzmaurice children grew up in an area dotted with Fitzmaurice estates and castles. Lixnaw Castle, only a few miles from Bedford House, belonged to a Garrett Fitzmaurice who lived in the early part of the thirteenth century. Near the sea, again, not far from Bedford House stood the ruins of another Fitzmaurice castle which was destroyed in 1583; still another lay in ruins in the town of Listowel. Parson Fitzmaurice grew up in Duagh House, a huge estate about three miles north of Listowel, with seven brothers, three of whom became doctors, one a banker, one a schoolmaster in Listowel, and two successful farmers, and two sisters who married well, adding to the wealth and prestige of the family. Befitting this social standing, George was ordained a clergyman in the Church of Ireland, but practiced his ministry for only nine years, preferring to take up a life of "country gentleman." Breeding horses and cattle and racing greyhounds turned out not to be lucrative enough to maintain a wife and twelve children. To support his family, and to continue to live the life of a gentleman farmer, Parson George, over a period of years, sold off most of the 500 acres he inherited. By the time he died in 1891, there was little land to will to his wife. The future playwright was fourteen years old.

Mrs. Fitzmaurice and her children, in very straightened circumstances, moved from Bedford House which they could not afford, to a small farmhouse nearby, where they lived as tenants. From this time on, the Fitzmaurice children were exposed primarily to the O'Connor side of the family rather than to the Fitzmaurice. The O'Connors were true Kerry peasants, and it is from these relatives that Fitzmaurice learned so much.[4]

At the time he [Fitzmaurice] wrote, Duagh was one of the last places in North Kerry to lose the Irish language. At the turn of the century the people with whom he grew up were moving from the Irish language into English for the first time and this is tremendously important. Therefore they were speaking Irish in their minds and translating it in their speech, which made them blunder sometimes into picturesqueness and he was wise enough to see this and to see how beautiful it was.[5]

At any rate, the effect of his parents' unconventional marriage was that George Fitzmaurice was a member in good standing of neither the gentry nor the peasantry.

In 1901 he began a forty year career as a clerk in a Dublin government office. The anonymity of the civil service suited George. During all these years he never made a friend. Nora

Kelley, who wrote a dissertation on George Fitzmaurice in 1973, interviewed several co-workers who corroborate this assertion. One such worker, John Hughes, describes Fitzmaurice as excessively shy, a stooped man with downcast eyes, a man who would say good morning when he arrived for work and very little else all day. William O'Connor, another fellow clerk, called Fitzmaurice the most self-effacing man he had ever met, very closemouthed and very unsociable. Another official, Joseph Finn, agreed: Fitzmaurice was a small, stooped man who always worked alone. He never attended any office parties. Fitzmaurice retired from the Department of Agriculture on his sixty-fifth birthday in 1942, and then lived as a recluse for the next twenty-one years in rented rooms in the heart of Dublin.

His life outside the office was not very different from his behavior at work. He attended Abbey plays in the theater's early years, and then in the 1920s began to frequent the music halls. But aside from these outings and a nightly visit to a neighborhood pub, Fitzmaurice had no social life. When he left his boardinghouse it was to visit the public readings rooms of the library to read newspapers or to enjoy his daily stout—always alone. In the last decade of his life, amazed that he had lived so long, and worried that his money would not outlast him, he began cooking his meals over a gas burner rather than eating in restaurants. Occasionally, he had visitors: a Kerry cousin on his mother's side, Minnie Mulcaire and second cousins on his father's side, Colonel Wilfred Fitzmaurice and his wife Marjorie. Shortly before he died he inherited the family farm at Kilcarabeg, and sold it to the man who had been running it for a pittance. He hoped that this new capital, added to his pitifully small pension would keep him: "He was a very proud man and would accept no assistance, saying he had plenty, though he lived in very poor circumstances."[6] George Fitzmaurice was, to his dying day, a very shy man, and although proud of his family name, he was very uneasy with those he considered moved in a higher strata of society; yet he was unable to find anything in common with the people he met at work or in the neighborhood pubs. They drove him more and more into himself.

He wrote plays and stories continually throughout his long government career, but exactly what and when is a matter of conjecture. After his Abbey production of 1923 (*'Twixt the Giltinans and the Carmodys*), twenty years passed before another of his plays was produced. Fitzmaurice was almost forgotten, except for the occasional appearance of a play in *The Dublin Magazine*. In the last twenty years of his life, there were a few semiprofessional and amateur performances of his plays.

His small success probably heightened his tendency to shyness. Even fellow writers like Seumas O'Sullivan and Austin Clarke often had difficulty locating Fitzmaurice, for he would drop out of sight for long periods of time. Austin Clarke tells that when he tried to revive an interest in Fitzmaurice in the 1940s, he received little encouragement from the author: "I met him occasionally and once or twice suggested the possibility of putting on *The Dandy Dolls*. But he was content with his quiet life and did not want any fuss or publicity.... I begged him to let me put on his strange play.... At last my patience was rewarded. On two successive Sundays, the second and ninth of December, 1945, the Lyric Theatre Company presented . . . *The Dandy Dolls*."[7] Unfortunately, the author was too ill at ease in public to be present.

It is known that Fitzmaurice's extreme reticence was responsible for certain of his plays not being staged. Howard K. Slaughter tells, for example, of certain correspondence found in his room after his death. On the torn off inside cover of an issue of *The Dublin Magazine* was this note to the earl of Longford, the Gate Theatre producer: "Some good while ago your Lordship was good enough to send me a note re a play called "The Enchanted Land" which appeared in *The Dublin Magazine*. It is regretted that a reply was not sent to your Lordship when the note was received, as it afterwards got mislaid. I daresay your Lordship has forgotten all about it. If not and if you still care to put on the play at your theatre I should of course be very glad if you did so."[8] This was written six years before he died, yet was found unsent though the play had never been produced. Also discovered was an unmailed letter to the earl of Longford's widow.

Excuse my approaching your ladyship re a three act play of mine which appeared in the Dublin Magazine for January - March 1957. Shortly afterwards the late Earl of Longford sent me a letter offering to produce the play which is called The Enchanted Land. Needless to state if I had been my normal self I should have jumped at the offer especially in a theatre of the Gate's reputation and also not for years had there been a production of any of my plays. But at the time I was suffering from an attack of acute neurosthenia to which I am subject and renders me on occasions, a border-line case. About the same time Radio Erin asked to be allowed to give a representation of *The Country Dressmaker* on its fiftieth anniversary to which I was also remiss in sending an answer. ... Afterwards I came to the conclusion to furnish His Lordship with the explanation given above but the lamented demise of your late husband, prevented me from doing so. Of course, Your Ladyship may never have read the play or alternatively if you had done so it might not have been the kind of play you would have put on. In that case no harm is done except whatever trouble I may by writing have put your Ladyship to in explaining what very likely appeared as very bad manners on my part.[9]

Fitzmaurice died in 1963 at the age of eighty-seven in a small room located near St. Stephen's Green. His possessions amounted to some clothes, copies of his plays, and miscellaneous papers, one of them a note scribbled in pencil: "Author is prepared to sell outright all rights in 14 plays[10] dealing intimately with life in Irish countryside. Most have already been either produced or published. Suitable to which to build musical, television, etc. Pass to anyone interested."[11] There were ten mourners at his funeral—three cousins and various representatives of the Dublin literary establishment.

In his last years Fitzmaurice refused to discuss his work, and he severed all contact with the world. Even at the beginning of his career he was reclusive, preferring pubs and music halls to literary gatherings of Yeats and his followers. He would also vanish to the west country for long spells of writing. It is not surprising then that such a man achieved no fame in the gregariously competitive Dublin literary market.

Undoubtedly there are other equally depressing stories from the years of the Irish literary revival, when new playwrights were springing up far too plentifully and subsiding into well deserved obscurity. Fitzmaurice, though, should not be unknown. He is a remarkable writer, a great original among folk dramatists, and an innovator of more than national interest.

II *Early Critics*

Despite his obscurity, Fitzmaurice always had some support in Ireland. Andrew E. Malone in 1929, in his history of Irish drama, called Synge, Lady Gregory, Colum, and Fitzmaurice the greatest of the Irish folk dramatists. Austin Clarke in 1940 in an article in *The Dublin Magazine* said that "the precarious difficult art form" in which Fitzmaurice experimented was the reason he was neglected and not, as he wrote much later in his edition of Fitzmaurice's fantasies, Yeats' jealousy. Padraic Colum in an interview in New York in March, 1964, said: "We should have forced Yeats and Lady Gregory to accept Fitzmaurice as they forced Dublin to accept Synge."[12]

III *Fitzmaurice and the Abbey's First Two Decades*

William Butler Yeats' interest in the revival of an Irish literature led him to the theater. As a poet he experimented over a long period of time, hoping to unearth new ways for the poet to find his place once more in the theater. Yeats felt the inferiority of naturalistic drama partly because it concerned itself with commonplace happenings and not with insights and passions, and partly because it reduced speech to emotionless words, thereby erasing the one indispensable characteristic of all literature — beautiful, vivid, even exuberant language.

It was John Millington Synge, and not Yeats, who fully succeeded in converting these poetic dreams to reality. But Synge died in 1909, and with his death the project of a poetic theater seemed doomed, since the Abbey continued to present realistic plays. New playwrights like William Boyle, Padraic Colum, Lennox Robinson, T. C. Murray, Frederick Ryan, Rutherford Mayne, and Seumas O'Kelley appeared, writing mainly of the towns, and in a naturalistic way. Yeats saw his dream of poetic drama at the Abbey receding in the distance.

At just this time George Fitzmaurice came to the Abbey. He seemed able to reconcile the new tendency toward realism with the initial movement toward poetic drama. His first play, *The Country Dressmaker*, owed much to Synge both in spirit and structure. The characters spoke with a richness formerly heard only from Synge. In the plays immediately following, *The Pie-Dish* and *The Magic Glasses*, Fitzmaurice's realism was blended with the colorful fantasy of Synge's and Lady Gregory's world. Yet in these plays the fantasy is mingled with a reality harsher than that of his forerunners; the romance disappears, leaving only the cold reality of an indifferent world. His "heroes" are peasants whose lives are constricted by fear of priest, neighbor, and the supernatural. All speak a language strongly regional, raucously poetic. Nevertheless, Fitzmaurice's fantasy, *The Dandy Dolls*, was rejected by Yeats and Lady Gregory, and the publication of his later plays went unnoticed.

"A drama of energy, of extravagance, of phantasy, of musical and noble speech," is part of Augusta Gregory's and William Butler Yeats' 1897 manifesto introducing the Irish Literary Theatre.[13] These words describe the kind of drama the founders were seeking, and yet, though they also describe *The Dandy Dolls*, Yeats and Lady Gregory refused to stage the play. At the time of the rejection of *The Dandy Dolls*, Yeats, full of discouragement because of the direction in which the Abbey was headed, announced he was ready to abandon a notion of a people's theater in favor of a select, aristocratic little theater.

"We hadn't the genius of Synge, his genius of combining poetry of speech with humdrum facts, and, of course, we hadn't the poetry of Yeats,"[14] Lennox Robinson has written of the second Abbey decade. Yet in the innovative plays of George Fitzmaurice they all ignored a drama of rich fantasy. It is impossible to account precisely for this rejection. The neglect of Fitzmaurice seems to have been the result of bad timing rather than of any personal antagonism or deliberate oversight. *The Country Dressmaker* was produced in October, 1907. *The Playboy* riots had occurred only a few months previously. Shortly after the riots, Ben Iden Payne, an English manager, was brought to the Abbey by its benefactress, Miss A. E. F. Horniman. He lasted for a very unpleasant six months, and then returned to England. The actors Willie and Frank Fay resigned just a few weeks after the opening of *The Country Dressmaker* amid much ill-feeling on all sides. *The Pie-Dish* appeared in March, 1908, as a curtain raiser to *The Golden Helmet*, and partly because of its unheroic subjject which contrasted with Yeats' heroic farce, and partly because of its confusion of moods, the audience disliked the play. *The Magic Glasses* was put on by the "second company" during a period devoted to productions of Gerhart Hauptmann, August Strindberg, and Rabindrangth Tagore, while the Abbey toured the United States.

But by then Fitzmaurice had lost faith. Overshadowed from the beginning by Synge's greatness and the battle of *The Playboy*, coming to the Abbey at a time when it was experiencing horrendous internal infighting, writing innovative drama with no explanation, and enjoying a stout by himself in a pub rather than socializing with the likes of Seumas O'Sullivan and Austin Clarke, who sought him out, George Fitzmaurice did not have a chance for fame. And without realizing it, Yeats had lost a valuable ally in his losing battle against the Abbey realists.

Fitzmaurice is an interesting dramatist, as a few critics have intimated. Even so, he has been almost totally ignored. One reason for the neglect has been a lack of a collected work. Now that his plays have been published as an entity, there is an opportunity to study them. Fitzmaurice wrote seventeen plays in all: nine realistic plays and eight folk fantasies. Much of his literary achievement was undervalued in his lifetime, and has been forgotten since. It is an unjustified neglect. His is talent, not genius, yet his best things, notably his fantasies, are minor classics.

CHAPTER 2

The Abbey Theatre and George Fitzmaurice as Short-Story Writer

G ENERALIZATIONS on national character tend toward exaggeration. Even so one can safely attribute to the Irish the idiosyncrasy that they have always been engrossed in the projection of their dreams and fantasies; in other words, they possess an inborn theatricality. No people has so consistently demonstrated the truth of Shakespeare's metaphor from *As You Like It* that "all the world's a stage, and all the men and women merely players." Is it not odd then that the Irish did not produce a native theatrical tradition?

I   *The Early Irish Stage*

From the seventeenth to the twentieth century, Ireland was a colony of England, politically as well as culturally. There was an Irish theater in Dublin and in smaller cities, but that theater was indisputably English. The Irish never presented their own life on the stage, and to chance upon an Irish produced play with the scene set at home was rare. William Smith Clark in *The Early Irish Stage: The Beginnings to 1720* writes that the reason for this was the "exclusively rural pattern of Gaelic culture which prevented the growth of an indigenous formal drama. Such drama everywhere has been the product of communal living, has been a town art supported by fixed patronage." But the Irish never founded a town. The towns and cities of Ireland are of Danish, Norman, or English descent. It was in these communities that regular dramatic entertainment arose out of immigrant English influence. "Hence the history of the stage in Ireland is the account of alien forces slowly molding and developing the

22

natural theatrical instincts in the Irish genius."[1] The Irish themselves found an outlet for their dramatic impulse in storytelling.

Even though Dublin had a theater as early as 1637, there was nothing that could be called an Irish dramatic tradition. Moreover, the theater of 1637 had been formed not by Irishmen but by the English conquerors; Irish writers with ambition in the theater went to London and of course established themselves as English, not Irish, writers. So it was in 1876 a twenty-year-old Dublin clerk named George Bernard Shaw left Ireland in order to become a writer—and so too had William Congreve in the seventeenth, George Farquhar and Oliver Goldsmith in the eighteenth, and Richard Sheridan in the nineteenth century.

At the same time Bernard Shaw was establishing himself in London, there was a noticeable trend, international in scope, toward scientific studies of folklore and myth which culminated in Sir James Frazer's *The Golden Bough* (1890). The "Celtic revival" which these studies spawned was essentially a discovery of the folk spirit, a spirit which is characterized by heightened passions and superstitions common to all literature rising from the peasant. In the 1890s in Ireland, still very much under English rule, there occurred an upsurge of interest in the epics of Ireland's ancient heroic past, recently translated by Celtic scholars. Part of the reason for this new interest in Irish history and literature was to find consolation for the fall of the great nationalist hero Charles Stewart Parnell;[2] and part of the reason was the Celtic revival itself.[3] Folklorists like Douglas Hyde taught themselves the Irish language (Gaelic) still spoken by the peasantry along the west coast of Ireland, and discovered a storehouse of legends. They also discovered that people whose first language was Gaelic spoke an uncommonly musical and vivid English. None of this might ever have gotten beyond the scholarly folklore journal had there not come together in time and place several men and one woman with the vision and genius to translate it all into a drama of universal appeal.

II   *The Abbey Theatre*

It was in 1898 that Lady Augusta Gregory, then forty-three, recorded in her diary a meeting with William Butler Yeats, then thirty-three. "He is very full of playwriting. He . . . is very keen about taking or building a little theatre somewhere in the suburbs to produce romantic drama." Yeats, born in Ireland, had been collecting Irish fairy tales, and though he was living in London at this time, he did not like big cities; moreover, he favored the peasantry who were, he thought, in close contact with the spiritual world. As early as 1893 he had written:

In one of his unpublished watercolour illustrations to Young's 'Night Thoughts', William Blake has drawn a numberless host of spirits and fairies affirming the existence of God. Out of every flower and every grass-blade comes a little creature lifting its right hand above its head. It is possible that the books of folk-lore, coming in these later days from almost every country in the world, are bringing the fairies and the spirits to our study tables that we may witness a like affirmation, and see innumerable hands lifted testifying to the ancient supremacy of imagination. Imagination is God in the world of art, and may well desire to have us come to an issue with the atheists who would make us 'realists', 'naturalists', or the like.[4]

By the time of his meeting with Lady Gregory in London in 1898, Yeats had already written *The Land of Heart's Desire*, a play about an Irish girl who is carried off to a "land where even the old are fair."

Of that meeting Lady Gregory records: We sat there through that wet afternoon, and though I had never been at all interested in theatres, our talk turned to plays. . . . I said it was a pity we had no Irish theatre where such plays could be given. Mr. Yeats said that had always been a dream of his, but he had of late thought: it is an impossible one, for it could not at first pay its way, and there was no money to be found for such a thing in Ireland.
    We went on talking about it, and things seemed to grow possible as we talked, and before the end of the afternoon we had made our plan. We said we would collect money, or rather ask to have a certain sum of money guaranteed. We would then take a Dublin theatre and give a performance of Mr. Martyn's [Edward Martyn] *Heather Field* and one of Yeats' own plays, *The Countess Cathleen*. I offered the first guarantee of £25.[5]

A few days later Yeats and Lady Gregory met again, in Ireland this time, in order to compose and mail a letter to raise funds for what they called the Irish Literary Theatre, a society devoted to the fostering of a native, poetic drama. "We propose to have performed in Dublin, in the spring of every year certain Celtic and Irish plays, which whatever be their degree of excellence will be written with a high ambition, and so to build up a Celtic and Irish school of dramatic literature."[6]

And so because Irishmen began to awaken to the long neglected legacy of Gaellic culture, Irish dramatic genius could be nurtured on native soil. The beginning of an indigenous Irish drama is due to the efforts not only of William Butler Yeats and Lady Gregory, but also to Edward Martyn[7] and to George Moore[8] who also helped found this Irish Literary Theatre.

Yeats and Martyn went to Dublin to obtain a theater. The only Dublin theaters, the Gaiety, the Royal, and the Queens, were booked far in advance. Then they discovered that no theatrical performance could be given for money in any building unlicensed for drama. In spite of these impediments, the first performance took place on May 8, 1899, at the Ancient Concert Rooms. Edward Martyn's *The Heather Field* and Yeats' *The Countess Cathleen* were presented. The first performance was so successful that the major London newspapers sent critics to Dublin to review the plays. Max Beerbohm was among them, and his and other reviews were exceedingly favorable.

The Irish Literary Theatre existed for three years during which time plays by Yeats, Martyn, George Moore, and Alice Milligan were produced as well as the first play written in Irish, Douglas Hyde's *The Twisting of the Rope.* In spite of the society's great dramatic successes, during the entirety of its three-year experiment only professional English actors, engaged from London, were employed, because they were all that were available. The society's aim was to train Irish actors in order to be able to perform oftener than once a year.

At this time two brothers, William and Frank Fay, then living in Dublin, were devoting their spare time to performing little farces in coffeehouses throughout the city. As they wanted professional, not amateur status in the theater, they understood that they would be forced to emigrate. The brothers chose America rather than England, and had they not attended one of the performances of the Irish Literary Theatre, the famed Abbey Theater might never have been born. With great enthusiasm to found a school of acting in Ireland for an Irish theater, they went to see Yeats and Augusta Gregory. When the

Irish Literary Theatre Society was reorganized as the Irish National Theatre Society in 1902, it featured an all Irish acting company headed by the Fays.

In 1902 and 1903 truly remarkable plays were produced: Yeats' *The Hour-Glass, The King's Threshold,* and *Shadowy Waters,* Lady Gregory's *Twenty-five,* Padraic Colum's *Broken Soil,* and John Synge's *In the Shadow of the Glen.* In May, 1903, the Irish National Theatre Society went for the first time to London. The actors, all amateurs, all trained by the Fays, all with regular daytime jobs, managed to get away by asking their employers for a Saturday holiday. They left Dublin on a Friday night, arrived in London Saturday morning, played in the afternoon and evening at the Queen's Gate Hall, and were back at work Monday morning. The English reviews were sensational, and attracted the attention of a devoted patroness of repertory theatre, Miss A. E. F. Horniman. Impressed by the plays and the performance of the actors, she offered to build a theater in Dublin to house the company. She obtained what had been the old Mechanics' Institute in Abbey Street and converted it to a theater. She not only gave the free use of the theater to the theater society, but provided an annual subsidy for several years. A Dublin newspaper, *The Evening Telegraph,* writing on the first of November, 1910, summed up her contribution:

The fairy godmother of the Irish Dramatic Movement parts with the Abbey today. . . . It should not be forgotten that were it not for the aid given to the dramatic movement in its infancy by Miss Horniman the Irish drama and the Irish acting world would never have grown into the healthy existence they both now enjoy.

Miss Horniman was truly a fairy godmother to the present drama movement in Ireland. Her generous monetary help was the wand that waved it into the proud position it now holds in the eyes of the artistic world, and we here in Ireland should not forget the fairy. . . . The Abbey Theater . . . came into being, and up to today it has been endowed by this disinterested artistic English Lady, who must have spent over £13,000 in building up the Irish dramatic movement into the really fine achievement it has become under her generosity.

The Abbey Theatre opened on December 27, 1904 with the presentation of four short plays: Yeats' *Cathleen ni Houlihan* and *On Baile's Strand,* Lady Gregory's *Spreading the News,* and Synge's *In the Shadow of the Glen.* This opening night is one of great events in the history of world theater. A handful of playwrights bent upon a national theater was joined by a group of actors with the same goal; the plays were written for a playhouse in a tiny country and have since been presented throughout the world. The Abbey Theatre directors were not interested in the comedies of manners which were popular in England. The subject matter for Abbey plays had to be Irish. The plays almost always concerned some aspect of peasant life or Irish legend. The Abbey was thereby freed from the excessive contemporaneity that was in vogue everywhere else in European theater, and this freedom made possible Ireland's outstanding contribution to twentieth-century drama.

The effect of this success upon the leading participants was astounding: Lady Gregory, at the time of the Abbey founding, was in her late forties and had previously worked hard translating the old Gaelic sagas of her Galway neighborhood, yet from this time forward she revealed a considerable talent, if not genius, for comedy. John Synge, who had planned to devote his life to French literary scholarship, wrote a wild and superbly joyous drama out of Irish peasant life. The effect upon Ireland and the world is stated in an editorial of October 26, 1912, which appeared in the *Freeman's Journal*:

It is time the Dublin public pulled itself together and began to take a pride in its National Theatre, this theatre which has produced in a few years more than a hundred plays and a company of players recognized as true artists, not only by their fellow country men, but by critics of England and America. The Abbey Theatre has made it possible for a writer living in Ireland and writing on Irish subjects to win a position of equal dignity with his fellow-artist in London or Paris; it has made it possible for an Irish man or woman with acting ability to play in the plays of their fellow country-men, and to earn a decent living and win a position of equal respect with an English or continental actor.

Some of the Abbey's most famous actors and actresses worked with the Fays—(they left the Abbey over a dispute with its directors, Synge, Yeats, and Lady Gregory in 1908)—during the early years: Dudley Digges, Ernest Vaughan, P. J. Kelly, Maire Nic Shiubhlaigh, and Sara Allgood.

But the most important and far-reaching effect of the early successes and growing reputation of the Abbey was that the company had begun to attract a number of exciting new dramatists, among whom was George Fitzmaurice. Lady Gregory knew this when she said that "it is the existence of the Theatre that has created play-writing among us";[9] then she supported her assertion by naming Fitzmaurice, among others, who turned to playwriting only after seeing the work of the Abbey Theatre. Fitzmaurice himself told Maurice Kennedy that he was attracted to the theater because "everyone was writing plays."[10] Fitzmaurice wrote at a time when interest in folktales and language was high, and this influenced all he wrote, but that he chose to write drama is a direct result of the Abbey's prominence. This judgment is based on the knowledge that Fitzmaurice began his writing career with short stories.

III   Short-Story Writer

Thanks to the investigations of Professor Robert Hogan, it is now known that Fitzmaurice's early writing was not for the stage. Between 1900 and 1907 he wrote short stories for the popular weekly press — The Weekly Freeman and The Weekly Irish Independent and Nation. It is not surprising that Fitzmaurice chose the short-story form: though the Irish never developed a native theater for their inborn theatricality, at least before the twentieth century, they did produce a satisfying equivalent in storytelling. Ireland is, after all, still a hospitable home for a rich oral tradition and this probably accounts for the fact that Ireland has produced innumerable first-rate short-story writers but very few comparable novelists. It is very natural, then, for a beginning writer in Ireland to turn to the short story.

Fitzmaurice's stories, like his plays, are all folk tales drawn from his Kerry background. The first of his stories, "Peter Fagan's Veiled Bride," appeared in The Weekly Freeman in 1900. This was a popular journal published by a Dublin daily newspaper, The Freeman's Journal, chiefly for distribution outside of Dublin. The stories which appeared in The Weekly Freeman were generally simplistic and romantically sentimental, but even so most Irish writers got their literary start by publishing in journals like it. Thematically this first story foreshadows the plays: Peter Fagan is tricked into marrying the less attractive of two sisters "the upshot of which was that Peter became reconciled to Mary." Reconciling one's self to less than what one wants is a recurring theme throughout Fitzmaurice's plays.

His second story, "Maeve's Grand Lover," appeared in *The Irish Weekly Independent and Nation* in the same year as "Peter Fagan's Veiled Bride." In this story Fitzmaurice makes fun of the quality of most of the work which appeared in the same journals in which he was publishing his stories. Because of the romantic ideas she gleans from her reading of the *Family Speaker*, Maeve spurns her faithful fiance Jamesie Landers for the villainous valet Mr. Shandrum-Dandrum whom she thinks is a lord. The story ends as the country dressmaker burns all her *Family Speakers.*

"The Plight of Lena's Wooers" also appeared in 1900, followed by "Peter Praisin" and "The Disappearance of Mrs. Mulreany" in 1901, "The Bashfulness of Philip Reilly" in 1904, "Cupid and Cornelius" in 1906, "The Streel" and, finally, "The Crows of Mephistopheles" in 1907. The stories are all quaint, ranging from the tale of the cunning matchmaker who gets rid of his "angelic" daughter to the story of the simple Michael who expects a gun to scare off predatory crows by itself.

Of the nine stories which Fitzmaurice wrote, seven deal with matchmaking, courtship, and marriage customs. The two already considered prefigure longer plays. "Peter Fagin's Veiled Bride" is the genesis of *The Simple Hanrahans,* and "Maeve's Grand Lover" contains the rudiments of *The Country Dressmaker.* "The Plight of Lena's Wooers" places the mother in the role of matchmaker. Mrs. Magrath, as owner of twenty-five cows and a pair of horses, with six hundred pounds in the bank, is a woman of great substance. She must, therefore, marry her only child, Lena, to a well-to-do farmer. Accordingly, she corresponds with a number of eligible bachelors who agree to meet with the Magraths. Lena, in love with poor Martin Foley, captures all the prospective husbands before they reach her mother, and with the help of Martin, ties them up in the oats barn. Meanwhile, Mrs. Magrath, outraged by the bachelors' bad manners in standing her up, relents and allows Lena to marry Martin. On the way home from the wedding the trick is discovered. Unwilling to tamper with a wedding ceremony, Mrs. Magrath invites the "lost" bachelors "to take some nourishment," when all is forgiven.

"Peter Praisin" also deals with a marriage trick, this time played by the uncle of a shrew he would like to marry off in order to get rid of her. "She was wan lump of gall and wormwood and vinegar mixed, and in another month I'd be in my grave from her tongue." The uncle, Peter, sings his niece's praises day and night to Jaymony Macnamara whose curiosity to meet this "angel" is aroused. They meet briefly, Peter apparently reluctant to allow his treasure to be courted, and Jaymony is enchanted. He applies to the local matchmaker, Lanty Muldoon, to make arrangements for a marriage. The story ends with Peter dancing and laughing wildly, repeating over and over, "well, there's nothin' like praisin'; but all the praisin' in the world won't praise her away from Jaymony."

Fitzmaurice uses a siimilar trick in a much later story, "The Streel," with the added twist of tricking the trickster. This is the most complicated of the stories. Sylvester Dansell is a bachelor of fifty. He has a sister, Maura, who is forty-three and still unmarried not only because she is unattractive and slovenly, but principally because she has no dowry. She schemes with matchmaker Peter Halpin to trick Sylvester into selling the farm to her. Peter, "an artist in word pictures," persuades Sylvester that money is better than waterlogged land. Besides, he can keep a cow and stay with his sister on the farm—easier, Peter reasons, than owning the land with all its attendant headaches. His talk about the pleasures of a life of leisure win Sylvester over. Next the matchmaker tricks his cousin Martin Tobin into agreeing to marry Maura. Before the prospective couple meets, Peter coaches Maura in ladylike behavior, insisting she sit in a chair in her blue satin dress and not speak or move when Martin comes to call. All seems destined to end happily when Sylvester suddenly changes his mind about the farm. Sylvester outwits the matchmaker by bringing Martin Tobin home unexpectedly so he can see Maura in her natural state with "her coal-black hair flying every way, and falling disorganized threads over the yellowish face and neck, her clothes bedraggled and fixed on her anyhow, her unstockinged feet showing through her brother's broken, unlaced cast-off brogues." The marriage trick in reverse works; a marriage is prevented.

Two marriage stories do not employ matchmaking stratagem. "The Bashfulness of Philip Reilly," in which true love triumphs without a trick, is noteworthy only because Fitzmaurice presents his first "Yank" character. In several of the plays such a character is central to the plot, especially in *The Country Dressmaker* and in *The Green Stone*. The second story, "Cupid and Cornelius," is interesting because it is somewhat autobiographical. Cornelius is a widower of forty. Mageen is his servant girl who cares for his three children. Cornelius wants to marry her but fears being ostracized socially. He is especially concerned about what his highly connected brothers, one a priest, another a doctor, and the third a councillor, would say. Only when he learns that Mageen plans to emigrate to America does he propose to her. Unlike the social consequences of Fitzmaurice's own parents' marriage, this story ends happily with everyone reconciled and even pleased by the merger.

Only two of Fitzmaurice's stories dispense with the marriage theme. One, "The Disappearance of Mrs. Mulreany," is gently satirical of the neighborhood busybody. Donacha O'Donoghue, who fancies himself a poet, solves the mystery of why Mrs. Mulreany has not appeared in town for more than a week. Letting his imagination go, he concocts an explanation on the flimsiest of evidence: this woman, strong as a bull, wearied of her frail husband, has run off to America with the local grocer. Donacha's wife, like all other Irishmen, highly prizes the value of a poet. ". . . 'tis a fine thing to have a janius of a man; the childre'll benefit by hearin' his fine talk, an' by minding the school they won't have to depend on the bit o' the land, thank God." But the sudden reappearance of Mrs. Mulreany leaves Donacha deposed as poet.

Fitzmaurice's last story, an embodiment of the tendency of Irishmen to brood over difficulty rather than to seek ways of overcoming it, is his best. "The Crows of Mephistopheles" is the story of Michael Hennessy who has been bothered by crows for three years. He even dreams of crows, picturing their leader with a cloven foot, a sign according to Michael, that the crows are in league with the devil. He has tried various remedies for ridding himself of the unwanted creatures, finally planting a half dozen frightening scarecrows in his potato garden. Nothing works. Finally, in desperation, Michael goes to the neighborhood Big House and borrows a gun from its master. He carefully sets the loaded and cocked gun on his fence and waits for the crows to be shot dead. After a long vigilance, during which the crows fly around his garden as usual, he grabs the gun, still loaded and cocked, and stomps off to the Big House to complain about the gun's worthlessness. Hearing the story, the master cannot control his laughter. Michael, thinking he was deliberately given a defective gun, weeps bitterly. The master himself goes to Michael's potato patch and kills several crows, causing the others to take flight. The squire tells Michael that if he has any more trouble with crows, let him know and he will kill a few more.

On the surface this is an entertaining story of a Kerry farmer's ignorant simplicity. Nora Kelley, in her 1973 dissertation on Fitzmaurice,[11] calls the story an allegory. Foreign invaders have been called crows from the time of Queen Elizabeth, Miss Kelley states. Moreover, Irish natives have been slow to do anything about foreign conquerors even though their domination has lasted several centuries. Peasants are slow to act because characteristically they blame misfortune on God's will or on the devil or on the influence of the fairies, a holdover from their pagan inheritance. Those who are decisive and can lead almost always spring from families of the Protestant aristocracy—the squires of the Big House. Miss Kelley's interpretation seems plausible chiefly because "The Crows of Mephistopheles" is the only instance out of nine stories and seventeen plays in which Fitzmaurice did not specify a setting for the action of his story. Instead, he subtitled it "a study in simplicity." Could he have meant that Ireland is "a study in simplicity?"

After the Dolmen Press printed Fitzmaurice's collected stories in 1970, Augustine Martin, a critic for *The Irish Press*, wrote that "they would not merit republication if they were not by Fitzmaurice,"[12] implying that they have no worth as stories, but that they command attention only because they precede a talented playwright's more important work. Perhaps this judgment is a little harsh. If nothing else, these stories show evidence of the same uncanny knack for reproducing Kerry dialect that Fitzmaurice developed in his plays. This gift is evident in as early a story as "The Plight of Lena's Wooers":

I hear from a friend of yours that you have a daughter for marryin', and as I am the owner of the grass of forty cows fully shtocked, an' just lookin' out for the likes, I'll take a turn over to ye an' have a talk afther to-morra evenin'. I'll take the thrain to Lyre, an' thin walk to your place. I'll take no wan with me, for I think carryin' hayros and tratin' thim to make wan's matches is all bosh. I expict we'll be able to settle the matter nice and aisy among ourselves. Of coorse you know what I am an' what I amn't, an' what I have an' what I haven't, an' I know the same about you, though we didn't meet six times. I believe your daughter will soot me; from what I hear she's A1. What I want is a genoone farmer's daughter, though at the same time a bit refined. Well-befriended, wid plenty tin, an' a horseload ov common sinse. Thin she must have a fairly good workin' record, an' always was known to have worn respectable clothes, etcetera. There you have me. I have no more to say at present. Both of us are wise, an' we don't want rawmaish.

In this story, as in the others, Fitzmaurice goes to endless pains to reproduce the North Kerry dialect phonetically, but mercifully he eliminates much of this phonetic representation, while retaining the vividness of the dialect, in the plays.

Even allowing for their realistic dialect, Fitzmaurice's stories overall are not well written. In all the stories the narration and description are formal and stilted. Typical is the following passage taken from "The Bashfulness of Philip Reilly":

If the two girls had but the faintest notion of what was then passing through Philip's mind they would have been exceedingly amazed. As a matter of fact he was endeavouring to screw up enough courage to enable him to do what would have seemed to any one of the other men in the cabin at that moment the easiest thing in the world, and it would have been so to Phil but that he was suffering from a very common complaint not confined to any particular clime. In other words, our hero was in love! Yes, and he had guarded his secret with such assiduity that nobody ever suspected that this erstwhile jolliest of rural giants was troubled with anything of the kind.

Even a good story like "The Disappearance of Mrs. Mulleany," reiminiscent of Lady Gregory's *Spreading the News* and of Fitzmaurice's own *The Terrible Baisht*, contains far too many similar passages.

Though the stories are lighter in tone than the plays, though they are less well written than the plays, their dialogue, like that of the drama, is flawless. When constructing dialogue, Fitzmaurice's formal pose drops from him and he becomes the dramatist with an ear for conversation. Even so, it is his drama and not his stories which make him one of the most interesting writers to come out of the Irish Renaissance.

CHAPTER 3

The Quintessence of George Fitzmaurice, Dramatist

I Recurring Themes

Y EATS and Synge perceived that to find the strong things of life that would make drama emotionally uplifting, as it had once been in Elizabethan times, they must look to the peasant folk of Ireland, a people in whom there still remained a magnificent and fiery imagination. Synge did write plays which distilled the wildness, the primitiveness, the grimness, and the joyousness of this peasant life, but in so doing he disturbed most of his countrymen. Indeed, *The Playboy* caused a riot because there were some who thought that Irish character had been impugned. George Fitzmaurice's *The Country Dressmaker* was even harsher in its picture of the materialistic Clohesys, but no riot occurred. Yeats, in writing about *The Country Dressmaker*, indicated why he thought this was so:

The truth is that the objection to Synge is not mainly that he makes the country people unpleasant or immoral, but that he has got a standard of morals and intellect. They never minded Boyle, whose people are a sordid lot, because they knew what he was at. They understood his obvious moral, and they don't mind Fitzmaurice because they don't think he is at anything, but they shrink from Synge's harsh, independent, heroical, clean, windswept view of things. They want their clerical conservatory where the air is warm and damp.[1]

It was not true that the people did not mind Fitzmaurice, as was made obvious by the very bad reception of his next play, *The Pie-Dish*, and for that matter, of all subsequent plays. Though Yeats writes in the same letter that Fitzmaurice "wrote it with the special object of showing up the sordid side of country life," *The*

Country Dressmaker is one of the most revived of all Abbey plays.

II   *Irish Peasant Themes*

Fitzmaurice certainly did not write *The Country Dressmaker* in order to show up the sordid side of country life, but neither did he try to hide the less appealing sides of the Irish peasant. All through his work he faced issues considered very controversial in rural Ireland—religion, matchmaking customs, and peasant materialism.

Fitzmaurice showed how wrong Yeats was when he said the Irish intellect was romantic and spiritual. The mystical strain may, of course, be found in Ireland as in all other countries. Yet as Bernard Shaw has shown in *John Bull's Other Island*, there are Peter Keegans, but there are far more Matty Haffigans and Larry Doyles. Instead of romance or spirituality there is a deadweight of grasping materialism hidden under a thin veneer of superstition which is attractive to all who never try to get beneath it. If the fairies are "the good people," it is only because they cannot be accused of the voracious land hunger of their human neighbors.

Most Irish farms are very small, though most have enough acreage to support an average family. But traditionally Irish farmers give themselves over to the raising of cattle; and this grazing uses most of the available land. Thus the prevalence of pasturage is the chief reason for the land hunger of the peasants. Moreover, Ireland is a country where land has been almost the sole available resource—all of which goes far to explain the grasping materialism pervasive in twelve of Fitzmaurice's seventeen plays. In *The Waves of the Sea* Wise James Danagher's machinations to cheat Rich Danager of his rightful inheritance are not very uplifting, and yet because of the acquiescence and aid of his entire family, we can guess they are not very unusual, either. Similarly, Michael Clohesy in *The Country Dressmaker* is Machiavellian in his design to capture "wealthy" Pats Connor for one of his daughters. Significantly it is not only the scheming Clohesys who have their eyes on Pats' money, but Julia's mother as well. Though she did not think highly of Pats in act 1, in act 2 "when Pats buys the Halpin's farm and has built the slate house on it," she cannot stop praising him. This land hunger is all pervasive in *The Moonlighter*, a drama of the Land War of 1880s as it manifested itself in North Kerry. By extension, the land hunger is converted to a madness for gold in *The Green Stone*. Martineen Collopy's relatives find his magic green stone, which can predict the future, a nuisance, for it keeps Martineen from doing any work on the farm. When a rich American arrives to buy the stone, Thade Shemus, and even the seminarian, Jimeen, unable to locate the real stone, substitute a false one. What is valuable to Martineen's family is made very clear: the stone becomes valuable to them because someone, admittedly a bumbling fool, wants to pay real money for it. In the end the real stone is destroyed, leaving behind pots full of gold which, if not held tightly, fly away. Ironically, the characters are kept prisoners in a world of their own greed.

This grasping greed is the reason behind another Irish phenomenon, the late and loveless marriage. The average age for marrying among Irish countrywomen is about twenty-eight, and is said to be higher than in any country in the world; that of men is higher still. And there are many who never marry at all. (George Fitzmaurice had eleven brothers and sisters; neither George nor any of his siblings ever married!) For those who do marry, land and livestock are usually involved. Physical attraction is not a prime consideration; romantic love is a luxury of the landless. Fitzmaurice reflects this feature of "Irishness" honestly. An impetus to Wise James Danager's thievery in *The Waves of the Sea* is to set up Delia Danager for "that fine rich lump of a publican, Murteen Donohue." In *The Moonlighter*, Luke Carmody does his own matchmaking for his daughter Breeda, for "tis only me knows the value of her." Similarly, in *'Twixt the Giltinans and the Carmodys*, the Giltinans "sell" their daughter Bridie just as the Carmodys "sell" Madge. In *The Pie-Dish* we discover that even greater than Margaret's fear of the local priest is her concern over what Leum's pie-dish making will do to her children's chances of contracting a good marriage. And in *The Coming of Ewn Andzale*, the impetus to all of Mrs. Davenport's machinations and fantasizing is what to do about getting her two unmarried daughters prosperously married: "Girls in Ireland, young or old, and no matter how beautiful they may be, have no chance of getting married nowadays unless they have money."

This Irish insistence on lucrative matchmaking occurs time and again; it shows up in eleven of the seventeen plays, for

Fitzmaurice mirrors the Irish scene honestly and unflinchingly. Even so, this recurring motif is exceeded by renderings of a curious synthesis of paganism and Christianity. All over Ireland both the country folk and gentry hold certain superstitious beliefs. A good Catholic might well believe in the older magic and yet go to Mass with a clear conscience; a Protestant, while in theory superior to all superstitious practices, might still catch something of a fearful half belief from talking with servants, grooms, and fishermen. This commingling of Christian piety and pagan superstition is exemplified in *The Dandy Dolls*. Father James wants to stop the Hag of Barna from destroying Roger Carmody's newest doll, for then he will not steal the priest's poultry. Keerby, Father James' clerk, is astonished that a priest would have anything to do with "this man or his dandy dolls," for there is "devilment of course by them dandy dolls, and it well known that when Roger was a garsoon two black ravens would perch upon his shoulder every morning." The priest reprimands Keerby for being filled with "pagan pishogues" (superstitions), and then calls for Roger to fetch his dandy doll for "'tis said there is to be a battle about tonight, for if there is power in dolls to put you from stealing my geese, believe you me, I'll make a doll of it; in a manner I'm going to baptize it a good Catholic by the grace of God!"

Here again, Fitzmaurice reports a pervasive fact of Irish life, for this spirit of pagan beliefs mingled with Christian references can be found throughout the cycles of mythology and in the early poetry of the bards. William Butler Yeats, in *Irish Folk Stories and Fairy Tales*, tells of his childhood visits with a man named Frank who owned a weaving shop.

"Is it me! Arra, what 'ud I be afeared o' them for?"
"Sure they have no power over me."
"And why haven't they, Frank?"
"Because I was baptized against them."
"What do you mean by that?"
"Why, the priest that christened me was tould by my father, to put in the proper prayer against the fairies—an' a priest can't refuse it when he's asked—an' he did so. Begorra, it's well for me that he did—(let the tallow alone, you little glutton—see, there's a weeny thief o' them aiting my tallow—because, you see, it was their intention to make me king o' the fairies."
"Is it possible?"
"Devil a lie in it. Sure you may ax them, an' they'll tell you."[2]

This is so much a part of the Irish character that even a priest is not free from the power of fairy belief. In *The Moonlighter*, Peg Driscoll and Ellen Guerin alternate between saying Hail Marys and Our Fathers for their rebel sons and discussing forebodings they have because "On May Eve the Good People [fairies] were seen as thick as midges on our triangle field."

This dovetailing of what is pagan into what is Christian, a blending actually of superstition and dogma, a grasping material-ism and a very unromantic view of marriage are themes typical of all peasant drama, as well as Irish drama, because they reflect the actuality of peasant life. While these motifs are reflected throughout George Fitzmaurice's plays, they appear in the works of other Irishmen as well. Fitzmaurice's practice of incorporating these motifs in his plays establishes his peasant quality and his "Irishness."

III   *Themes Unique to Fitzmaurice*

Fitzmaurice, nonetheless, is very much his own man. A close reading of the plays reveals three themes basic and unique to Fitzmaurice: themes concerning compromised hopes, themes relating to the rebel who must stand alone, apart from his community, and themes analogous to an overall antiheroical vision of life, meaning a certain disparaging lampoon of all Fitzmaurice observes.

A theme that runs through most of his plays is a stoic acceptance of less than the ideal by putting up with second best. The central character of *The Country Dressmaker*, Julia Shea, has been faithful to Pats Connor, who returns from America after a ten years' absence. Julia is like Lydia Languish: she has idealized love out of all resemblance to actuality by reading romantic novelettes. She refuses Edmund Normyle because of her love for Pats; she then refuses Pats when she learns that he has not always been romantically faithful, but was once married. Finally she is persuaded to accept him, and with him, reality: "The spring of life is broken in me, but if it is your wish entirely, then I am willing to make the best of it."

Equally unromantic is the short peasant comedy, *'Twixt the Giltinans and the Carmodys*. For fifteen years Billeen Twomey has been unable to decide whether to marry Bridie Giltinan or Madge Carmody. After much plotting to snare him, both of the girls' families turn on him, resulting in one of Fitzmaurice's many stage fights. In the end Billeen makes the best of it by marrying Old Jane, a dour, middle-aged servant who discovers to her chagrin that Billeen does not possess the money she thought he did. At the very end the two decide to make the best of it. The stage directions pinpoint the profound sadness in compromised hopes: "Old Jane and Billeen move slowly towards one another, showing signs of antagonism rather than affection. They embrace grimly and determinedly, and a loud kiss is heard." The best of a bad thing is still pretty bad, even though this unromantic view is wryly embodied in farce.

Again, in *The Simple Hanrahans*, Fitzmaurice combines slapstick with his motivating idea that we must put up with second best. *The Simple Hanrahans* is a three act comedy about a family of farmers named Munnix who hope to trick the presumably simple Hanrahans into marriage of Pete Munnix with Lena Hanrahan. But it soon appears that the Hanrahans have already outwitted the Munnixes—and indeed, with other trades and bargains, everyone else in the neighborhood. Though the action is fairly slim and static, and much of the play's humor depends on embarrassingly overdone, never ending semi-malapropisms, there are a few amusing parts. On his wedding night, Pete Munnix discovers his bride has a wooden leg, false teeth, and no hair. There is nothing to be done, however, and after recovering from his initial shock Pete decides to accept Lena, and everyone else must be content. Here again is another instance of Fitzmaurice's observation that reality never matches expectation, and that the wise man must be content with reality, poor substitute though it is for the ideal.

Though *The Ointment Blue* is the most cheerful Fitzmaurice play, the nagging realization that actuality will never measure up to ideality is present here too. It is the story of the champion fighter of Carraweira, Dermot Rue Mullarkey, and a tournament that the king and queen of Ireland hold to determine who will marry their elder daughter. Dermot's previous prowess was derived from a little box of ointment given him by an old hag. His ointment however, has run out, and the attempts of his uncles,

Teig of the Trees and Donacha are not sufficient to prevent the
hag from giving the ointment to Cormac O'Rourke. At the
tournament there is another onstage fight which eliminates all
the heroes except Dermot and Cormac. Finally, although
Cormac defeats Dermot, Dermot does win the second daughter,
Roseen, and a legacy from her rich uncle in Texas. Though this is
not what Dermot wants, "a half of loaf is better than no bread."

This is the essential Fitzmaurice: life is not what we would like
it to be, so let us accept what is rather than pretend it is
something else. Such a view of life begets a basic tolerance for
flawed humanity. *The Moonlighter* deals with the troubled times
of the Land War, and contrasts the characters of Peter Guerin, a
"reformed" Fenian, and his son Eugene, a fiery patriot in words
only, against a background of the undercover revolutionary
activity of the time—activity which sometimes degenerates into
mere faction fights, and at other times is diverted to private
vengeance under the guise of patriotism. Peter's ardor has
cooled, and his contempt for the verbose school of patriotism
which his son represents is strong. When the old time spirit was
aroused, it was he, and not the word spinners, who translated
words into deeds. His son's good friend Tom has been trying to
escape the police for a week. There is a boat waiting for him, but
the police are on a bridge overlooking the boat. Suddenly Peter
remembers that these same police are "the black cowards that
shot down the men of Ireland when myself and his [Tom's]
Uncle Martin stood shoulder to shoulder in the Fenian days!" In
trying to help Tom, he is killed.

In this there is nothing soft; it is not vague or mawkish.
Fitzmaurice is not a sentimentalist. The true peasant is not
sentimental, and Yeats knew this, too. *In Plays and Controversies*
he described the disdain of a village shoemaker, a great reader,
for writers who sentimentalized the people and of the man's wish
for a literature which would show the people "in their naked
hideousness." Yeats concluded: "That is the peasant mind as I
know it, a mind that delights in strong sensations whether of
beauty or ugliness, in bare facts, and it is quite without
sentimentality."[3] Fitzmaurice tries to present life honestly,
imparting acceptance of what life brings. Instead of writing plays
of easy cheer, he wrote with this harsh quality, and he was not
accepted.

In his best plays he employs harshness with fantasy to

emphasize the pain of the artist-dreamer-escapist who finds himself in surroundings of indifference or incomprehension. *The Pie-Dish* presents the tragedy of Leum Donoghue, a man from a poor family who devoted his adult life to the conception and elaboration of a pie-dish. Infirmity and death came upon him before his masterpiece was completed. Leum's clay dish is a representation of the lost happiness of his early life and it is to be the final and complete expression of his artistic soul. But because of his pie-dish making, Leum is treated with contempt by his family, and in the end his precious object is destroyed. The real question is whether Leum understands fully what the pie-dish means. He thinks it is the masterpiece of his creative soul, but significantly, he has spent thirty years thinking about it, but could not execute his work of art because in all that time various diversions came between him and it. Does a real artist procrastinate? Is he not really hiding from life's unfulfilled promise? Is his pie-dish akin to Ibsen's "life-lie" or O'Neill's "pipe-dreams?" Is Leum an escapist or artist or both? There is a sense of pathos that rings out of *The Pie-Dish*: if Leum is an artist, he has produced no masterpiece; if he is an idle dreamer, he died with his "vital lie" intact, for no one knows "what was in the pie-dish at all."

And so also *The Dandy Dolls* may be interpreted as an allegory of the creative impulse struggling to express itself though frustrated by forces of poverty, ignorance, and superstition. Roger Carmody is an artist who puts the yearning of his artistic soul into the creation of his dolls. But he has to contend with a nagging wife urging him to domestic chores, with a philistine village and priest, and with the bogeywoman of legend—the Hag of Barna who with her devilish son steals the windpipes from the throats of the dolls. Roger took up the making of the dolls to keep himself home at night to distract himself from stealing and eating ducks and geese for which he has a violent passion. He regrets his lost youth and he attempts, like Leum Donoghue, to create or recall the beauty and perfection he does not find around him. As usual in a Fitzmaurice fantasy, things do not work out, for if he now makes dandy dolls all day long, he never quite achieves perfection, and with each failure remembers lost opportunities and breaks away again to chase ravenously after geese and ducks.

At the climax of the play word spreads that Roger has finished another dandy doll, and not only does the Hag's son plan an attack on the doll, but the Grey Man, one of the Coonihans of the Isle of Doon, Bauble-Makers to the king and queen of Spain, arrives. Roger's wife and child are hungry, and a leak in the roof need repairing. The priest enters to protest the stealing of his poultry and baptizes the latest doll in order to foil the Hag's Son; for Roger, like Leum, is suspected of being involved in his act with evil powers. Both the Hag and Son descend, the Coonihans join the battle along with the priest and everyone else until Roger is carried off by the Hag and her Son, after still another of Fitzmaurice's onstage fights, to their "woful den" in the Hills of Barna. His wife and child are well rid of him, and the priest's geese are safe from Roger's nightly raids.

One clue to what Fitzmaurice is getting at can be seen in the figure of the Carmody child—a character as remote from the action as the dolls themselves. Traditionally a prey of the supernatural in Irish folklore, the child on this occasion is ignored both by the parents and by the intruders. Their attention is transferred from the natural creation to the artifact. For Fitzmaurice the real child is the artist's protest against domesticity, in the sense that his presence forces real life to intrude upon Roger. It is the focus of the Irish artist's lonely battle against society at large: Roger must retreat to his shed to get his doll making done. His opponents are not merely the members of his own family (the child and Cauth), but the power of the church (Father James and Keerby), and the inheritance of his native culture (all the folk superstitions represented by the Hag and her son). The point of Fitzmaurice's use of a real child is to magnify what the doll is—a convenient symbol for any work of art. Different symbols for the same thing appear in Fitzmaurice's fantasies, usually specified in the title.

There is in *The Magic Glasses*, as in *The Dandy Dolls*, a criticism of a philistine public to which an artistic manifestation has all the appearance of deviltry. Jaymony, the poet, the dreamer, the musician, the visionary, the escapist, literally brings down the roof on his own head when he is unable to give up his endless dreaming. Jaymony is a middle-aged bachelor, and has stayed for more than twenty years in his parents' top loft where he gazes into magic glasses and sees wondrous things.

. . . the seven wonders of the world, seas and mountains and cities, grand horses and carriages, and all the wild animals of the earth. God and white money you'd see in heaps. Palaces, with the finest furniture inside of them, the best in eating and drinking laid out on tables with the loviest chaney .... Women. Full of the purtiest women was ever seen on the globe. It's myself got very fond of one of them, and maybe of two. And in the glass I could see myself and the one I was doting on, and we together for six days of the week. Times we'd be talking and times there wouldn't be a word out of us at all, our two mouths in one kiss and we in a sort of daze. ... Ah, but I seen more, for 'tis myself I see on a noble horse, spangled and grey; I see my own bright sabre flashing and I leading the army on, and we driving the Saxon invader before us—through the plains of Desmond, and on and on, even to the Eastern sea.

In Jaymony's story the extremes of the dream opposed to reality, of the dreamer versus the practical man are portrayed. Morgan Quille is summoned to cure Jaymony. He sets out to defeat Jaymony's magic with his own, outdoing his patient's visions with the great wonders of the world, tempting him to exchange his fantasies for a useful, practical life. Jaymony capitulates, but at the first intrusion of the real world, the coming of his brothers for a visit, he slips back to the safety of the loft where his betrayal of Morgan Quille's enchantment is punished by the collapse of the loft. Jaymony's jugular vein is cut by the magic glasses. The family, in fear of legal reprisal, rush out to call for the neighbors so they can see how Jaymony was killed by the debris of his own loft.

In this way the visionary is brought to ruin in Kerry. Using his imagination Jaymony constructed his own artificial world to compensate for the real one. And by extension, is not this what Fitzmaurice is doing with his work? However much Fitzmaurice sees the limitations of the real world, he constantly affirms the value of imagination. In fact, we can conjecture that he uses his imagination to turn what was distasteful to him into farce and fantasy. And, as Fitzmaurice implies, the dreamer must tell his dream even though it cannot be understood by others, and even though he suffers in the telling. The more the dreamer is derided the more closely does he hold his dream to himself. Eventually he withdraws from life completely, and for this he must pay a fearful price: Leum locks himself into an unbearable solitude by outlandish pie-dish making; Roger is abducted by destructive supernatural beings; Jaymony is literally destroyed in his retreat; and George Fitzmaurice continues to fashion his pie-dish and his dandy dolls and peer through his magic glasses, but all the while becoming ever more reclusive to the damage of his art. Fitzmaurice did not see many of his plays staged. For a dramatist, and most especially for one trying to experiment, this is disheartening. For, unlike other forms of literature, the drama is a collaborative medium; it is dependent upon many contributions besides the text itself.

In *The Green Stone* Fitzmaurice produced another variation on the same theme, this time telling the story of Martineen Collopy who has a magic green stone which lets him see into the future. But this play differs from its predecessors in the meaning of the symbol. A prophetic stone is obviously a valuable object, and even Martineen's obtuse family and neighbors can see that. The point of the previous symbols—the dolls, the pie-dish, and the glasses—is that they, like art itself, are absurd and useless, utterly impractical and indefensible to anyone who does not apprehend their value. In *The Green Stone*, as in *The Pie-Dish*, the emphasis is not on the artist struggling against conformity as much as on the dreamer criticizing the practical man.

In *John Bull's Other Island*, George Bernard Shaw may have gone to the root of what it is about men (such as Martineen, Jaymony, Roger, and Leum) that drives others crazy when he makes Larry Doyle pour out his embittered confession:

Oh, the dreaming! dreaming! the torturing, heartscalding, never satisfying dreaming, dreaming, dreaming, dreaming! No debauchery that ever coarsened and brutalized an Englishman can take the worth and usefulness out of him like that dreaming. An Irishman's imagination never lets him alone, never convinces him, never satisfies him; but it makes him that he can't face reality nor deal with it nor handle it nor conquer it; he can only sneer at them that do, and be 'agreeable to strangers' like a good for nothing woman of the streets. It's all dreaming, all imagination.[4]

Fitzmaurice's people suffer from the effect of this dreaming, and as a result there is an undercurrent of tragedy in the plays. But these people possess the grotesque symptoms without Larry Doyle's awareness of them, and as a result there is also much comedy in the plays. For one of the main differences between tragedy and comedy is that the tragic figure becomes truly tragic when he achieves self-knowledge; the comic figure becomes comic when he is unable or pretends to be unable to see his true self.

This may account for the fact that Fitzmaurice's fantastic characters are unheroic as well as comic. His "heroes" are blustering frauds or useless dreamers, and the supernaturals are every bit as foolish as the humans. Take Roger Carmody who has spent twenty years making his dolls, only to have every one taken by the "Barna brat" while the dollmaker hid under the bed, always "leaving the tussle to Timeen Faley," his friend "that's always to the fore!" Cauth, his wife, calls him "dirty mean and craven." He supports his family by stealing Father James' poultry. He lives only to create his dolls, and is "worse than a surly mastiff" if disturbed in his work. Gauth's call for him, "Roger—Roger—aboo—oo" echoes the Gaelic war cry, a buaid, "to victory," a call associated with great battles—here ironically pointing to his antiheroic ways. At the end of the second scene, after the Hag's son has taken the doll while Roger watches cowering in the corner, he gives up all concern. "But to hell with everything, I don't care, and by damned I'll have a goose." And none of the other characters is any better. The Grey Man, one of the three feared Grey Men of Doon, sounds ominous enough, but when he comes to warn Roger what will happen if he loses his most recent doll, he spends half of the time flirting with Roger's old, wrinkled wife. Quilter of *The Country Dressmaker* and Quille of *The Magic Glasses* are both imaginative rogues, comic and totally unheroic. In *The Green Stone* the magical mermaid must "catch a hold of her tail and rowling over the land like sixty, and hop and bump like a football over ditches and hedges and all" crying "gay-gay" to attract attention. The cowards and antiheroes abound in Fitzmaurice's work: Billeen Twoomey in *'Twixt the Giltinans and the Carmodys* who cannot commit himself to marriage, the farmers and townspeople in *The Terrible Baisht* who are intimidated by a tinker, Padden in *The Magic Glasses* who wants to hide when Mr. Quille comes to cure Jaymony, and even Eugene Guerin in *The Moonlighter* who despite his fiery patriotic words, is shown to be spiritless and fainthearted. Fitzmaurice's whole vision is antiheroic. Once Austin Clarke asked Fitzmaurice to tell him about the folk about whom he had written his plays. Fitzmaurice replied, "They are wicked old children."[5] At the same time he told Clarke that *The Linnaun Shee* was a satire on Yeats and his cult of the fairies.[6] But in all fairness to Yeats, in such early poems as "The Stolen Child," "The Hosting of the Sidhe," and "The Happy Townland," all written long before *The Linnaun Shee*, he is becoming more and more aware of the dangers of the fairy world as well as its attractions. The fairy world for Yeats represents a pull away from everyday life, an escape from duties, but it is also the "world's bane."

The Linnaun Shee deals again with the lost joys of youth, this time as regretted by a middle-aged Kerry farmer. Jamesie Kennelly is neither visionary nor artist, but he is at that critical age when he must put early ideals behind him and settle down to his lot. Although Jaemsie is fifty-five he has lately begun to consort once more with the Linnaun Shee who had held him bewitched until the day he married. The Linnaun Shee is the female fairy lover who make passes at young men and lightens the grey agricultural existence of the Kerry peasant. No doubt such beliefs were and are still current in the countryside, and Fitzmaurice has used them dramatically with sly fun.

As a result of Jamesie's middle-aged madness the farm has fallen into neglect and his domestic life is getting out of hand. Lately Hanora, his wife, has discovered that his thoughts are again turning to the fairy woman, and she dreads the approach of May Eve,[7] when the Linnaun Shee is to take him away. When she does arrive, she appears as a horrid hag, but to Jamesie she is a beautiful young girl and he goes with her. This is very like Yeats' *Cathleen ni Houlihan*; in both plays there is an entrance of an old hag whose lover sees her as beautiful, and who follows her into the night.

Jamesie goes out with the Shee who chants "come away, come away." After some obscurely violent climax, Jamesie reappears alone. He looks "queer and haggard"; he is obviously free of enchantment. Having survived the experience, Jamesie, returns to the cottage full of practical plans for improving the farm. But it is clear that something has gone irreparably from his world. The ineffectual dreamer must settle down to agricultural everydayness.

So Fitzmaurice is half of the side of the enemy. His men of imagination are not lonely heroes upholding a noble cause; they are fools and their sacrifice is worthless. There may be conflict, but there is no hope for either side: all share the plight of the farmer in Fitzmaurice's short story, "The Crows of Mephistopheles," who tried to clear his land of crows by taking a loaded gun into the field and waiting for it to go off. In the first sentence of this story is the observation: "A tendency to upbraid fate—to brood over misfortunes rather than to immediately seek by what means they may be palliated or overcome—seems to be generally characteristic of the Celt." So it does, and his plays are deeply rooted in this tendency.

Fitzmaurice never takes refuge in the artificial happy endings characteristic of other writers. (The only exception, out of seventeen plays, is *The Coming of Ewn Andzale*, an anagram for "the coming of New Zealand," which deals with the wish-fulfillment fantasy of the emigrant relative returning laden with money. Significantly, this is Fitzmaurice's worst play.) Like other Abbey dramatists, he built his plays around miracles and magic, but unlike the others, he never offered these as spiritual consolation. Over and over again we get the same ideas in his plays—that life is not what we desire and we must make the best of it. Fitzmaurice is concerned with idealism and aspiration as they stand opposite reality and human limitation. The plays do not show the two extremes in conflict, but rather that in Kerry, anyway, the ideal has not much chance. The artist is stifled by the pressing demands of surviving on a small farm. Possibly, overall, Fitzmaurice was concerned with the plight of the disowned or disinherited artist, his own plight really: the dreamer and his shattered dream. Fitzmaurice writes of a particular man in a particular place: the Kerry idealist whose inspiration is undermined. And this, despite the pervasive farce and fantasy, accounts for the harshness of Fitzmaurice's world.

IV   *Language*

One of the chief propositions, made in the 1897 manifesto inaugurating the Irish Literary Theatre, was that a drama of beautiful language could be born in Ireland because of the Irishman's passion for words, talk, language, and even oratory. The characters of Irish drama are themselves filled with the joyous possibilities of talk. Synge's Nora, in *The Shadow of the Glen*, is impressed with the exhuberant speech of the tramp: "but you've a fine bit of talk, stranger, and it's with yourself I'll go." Pegeen tells Christy Mahon in *The Playboy of the Western World*: "any girl would walk her heart out before she'd meet a young man was your like for eloquence, or talk at all." And Michael Miskell in Lady Gregory's *The Workhouse Ward* whimpers: "All that I am craving is the talk. There to be no one at all to say out to whatever thought might be rising in my innate mind! To be lying here and no conversible person in it would be the abomination of misery." A person who can talk eloquently is admired and even envied. Aeneas Canty in George Fitzmaurice's *The Ointment Blue* is pompous, but he can outtalk Polonius. Donacha, "in angry astonishment and with unwilling admiration" says "Glory be to the Almighty God, Teig, but it's like out of a machine they [words] rowl from him." Teig "contemptuously" retorts: "Whist with you! Wait till I'm Minister of Justice and my opportunity—things will come from me will put that fella in the halfpenny place." Similarly, John Daly, the grocer in *The Terrible Baisht*, who has caused all sorts of trouble by his exaggerations, is quite proud of his imaginative fancies: "The terrible baisht! The ductil dolimoo! The beano at Mount Eagle! I must surely be some sort of poet."

Throughout Fitzmaurice's plays there appear and reappear certain types outstanding for this verbal proficiency: the hustler like Teig of the Trees, the braggart like John Daly, matchmakers like Malachi Cantillon and Luke Quilter and Michael Clancy, and wonder-worker-rogues like Morgan Quille and the Grey Man. In each play there is a professional talker, a man who by virtue of his eloquence controls events or at least tries to keep things moving.

In *The Toothache* it is Jim who organizes the action and persuades Patsey Dunn to spend more money on porter than he would have spent on a good dentist—and all without Patsey's awareness of any trickery. Luke Quilter, the man from the mountains in *The Country Dressmaker*, can talk circles around any other character, and because of this he is the matchmaker. In *The Ointment Blue* Teig of the Trees is the poet and commands attention because of his verbal ability. But he gets a great deal of competition from Aeneas Canty, and he is very jealous as a result. In *'Twixt the Giltinans and the Carmodys* it is Michael Clancy's word wizardry that finally impels middle-aged Billeen Twomey to get married. In certain characters, like Delia in *The Waves of the Sea*, Fitzmaurice can differentiate poses. Skillfully, he contrasts Delia speaking pretentiously and Delia speaking naturally.

But, Aunt Halligan how I wish you had been with us in London. . . . We went to Dublin of course—we spent three days there—a gossipy little place, Dublin—and such droll people. I wouldn't mind, Wise James, if the accent only remained with me until tomorrow itself and I going to Listowel for the sole purpose of having one good crow over that scut Maimie McCarthy after the show and the laugh she made of me last year below in Limerick before all the clerks inside in Cannock's because I said 'tay' instead of 'tea.'

This is not the only place Fitzmaurice exposes affectation in language. The rich extravagance of much of his peasant speech gives way in *The Simple Hanrahans* to malapropisms repeated over and over by nearly every character. The device is exceedingly overused. Billy Roche, a process server, tries to use polysyllabic words he thinks befit his prestigious job. Jaymary Gunn, the pompous national teacher, corrects Roche's obvious mistakes. The fun is supposed to occur for the reader or the audience in watching Gunn trip up on word meanings as well. The fact that these two "go at it" all through three long acts is bad enough, but incredibly, most of the other characters indulge in the excesses, too. Here is an instance where Fitzmaurice, drunk with the possibility of word play, carried away by malapropisms and misuses of foreign languages, satirizes affectation in language, and in the process becomes guilty of affectation himself.

In any event, whether his verbal artifice is excessive or not, Fitzmaurice often portrays a hero-rogue-poet, a man for whom everything is talk, and this language trait is directly attributable to the Irish music-hall tradition and to Victorian dramatist Dion Boucicault's rendering of that tradition in his plays.

V   *Music Hall and Boucicault Influences*

We know that Fitzmaurice was a devotee of the music hall. *One Evening Gleam* is nothing but the dialogue of three tenement women reminiscing about the Dublin music halls. Colonel Fitzmaurice, a cousin of the playwright, confirms George's lifelong fondness for music halls.[8] Maurice Kennedy, probably the only person to interview Fitzmaurice, writes that the dramatist spoke lovingly of the "great days of the old-time music hall."[9] And Austin Clarke wrote in 1967 that Fitzmaurice "had not been in a theater for more than thirty years and went only to music hall shows."[10] "When George Fitzmaurice felt that he had been thrust from the romantic movement by the founders of our National Theater, he became a devotee of the Music Hall and consoled himself as best he could in watching a comic tradition which was rapidly declining. The snatches of jingle in his last fantasy, *The Enchanted Land*, may be regarded as an embarassing concession to popular taste."[11] Howard K. Slaughter tells us that "During the years following the turn of the century, Fitzmaurice became—and remained all his life—an ardent admirer of music hall shows. This experience helped fashion his later career as a dramatist, just as it influenced O'Casey. Musical shows flourished at the Empire (later the Olympia) where one could see operas. ... There were pantomimes as well and street singers. At the Tivoli and the old Royal one could see the great Harry Lauder and other favorites perform. Tuppence secured the patron a seat in the gallery to see the shows."[12] Fitzmaurice's interest in the music hall never waned, and *One Evening Gleam* reflects over fifty year's interest in this entertainment.

Some of the Dublin pubs which Fitzmaurice frequented served as makeshift music halls, for they often presented live entertainment for their patrons. Singing comedians were the most popular. They carried on a series of running gags in the midst of their songs very similar to the routines of Jimmy Durante. Many of them carried on dialogues with a sidekick between the verses of a ballad. *The Toothache*, Fitzmaurice's first play, is a good example of how it was done: there is a dialogue between Jim and the rest of the characters, interspersed with Neddy the poet's ballad of "green brooms." This play illustrates the type of music-hall entertainment that Fitzmaurice knew and enjoyed.

Boucicault borrowed heavily from this tradition, and although Fitzmaurice's characters are far removed from Boucicault's stage Irishmen, and though Boucicault's facile humor is nothing like Fitzmaurice's harshness, there are similarities of language style. Boucicault's Irish plays, *The Shaughraun, The Colleen Bawn*, and *Arrah-na-Pogue* depend upon comic dialogue—the Irish wit and roguish blather with which their comic villains amuse and defend themselves. Synge, though he wrote little dramatic criticism, did suggest in the English magazine, the *Academy and Literature* (on June 11, 1904), that modern Irish dramatists should imitate Boucicault's rich speech. With his somewhat corny blarney, Boucicault's Shaughraun may be the essence of the stage Irishman, but he is also an archetype of Synge's

Playboy, O'Casey's Paycock, and Fitzmaurice's matchmakers and wonder-workers, whose humor is in their language. Part of the reason we like to listen to their words "rowl out like a machine" is the characteristic extravagance and exaggeration.

In Boucicault *The Shaughraun*, for example, Mrs. O'Kelly tells her son,, Conn, that the police have accused him of stealing Squire Foley's horse. Conn replies,

Well, here's a purty thing, for a horse to run away with a man's character like this! Oh, wurra! may I never die in sin, but this was the way of it. I was standing by ould Foley's gate, when I heard the cry of hounds comin' across the tail-end of a paycock, an' the finest dog fox you'd ever seen sailing ahead of them up the boreen, and right across the churchyard. It was enough to raise the inhabitants. Well, as I looked, who should come up and put his head over the gate beside me but the Squire's brown mare, small blame to her. Divil a thing I said to her, nor she to me, for the hounds had lost their scent, we knew by their yelp and whine as they hunted among the gravestones, when, wish! the fox went by us. I leapt on the gate, an' gave a shriek of a view halloo to the whip; in a minute the pack caught the scent again, an' the whole field came roarin' past. The mare lost her head, an' tore at the gate. 'Stop' ses I 'ye divil' and I slipped the taste of a rope over her head an' into her mouth. Now mind the cunnin' of the baste, she was quiet in a minute. 'Come home now' ses I, 'asy!' And I threw my leg across her. Be gabers! No sooner was I on her bare back than whoo! holy rocket! She was over the gate, an' tearin' like mad afther the hounds. 'Yoicks'! ses I; 'come back the thief of the world, where are you takin' me to?' as she went through the huntin' field an' laid me besides the masther of the hounds, Squire Foley himself. He turned the colour of his leather breeches. 'Mother of Moses!' ses he, 'is that Conn the Shaughraun on my brown mare?' 'Bad luck to me!' ses I, 'It's no one else!' 'You stole my horse', says the Squire. 'That's a lie!' ses I, 'for it was your horse sthole me!'

The speech of one of Fitzmaurice's verbally prodigal scoundrels, Moran Quille, (*The Magic Glasses*), is like Conn's dialogue in a very important way in that both use comic rhetoric to defend and to beguile, and both are masters of the art. After all, men like this survive by their verbal prowess. Granted, the two speeches are not alike in sound and syntax: note Boucicault's "ses I", and "ses he" in contrast to Fitzmaurice's more formal dialogue:

Twenty miles of a tramp to cure a boy with a breast bone down! Twenty miles, and starting with the streak of dawn! Yet there's devils would say the fame of Morgan Quille would never pass the bounds of Beenahorna—doctors, priests, and jealous devils would say Morgan Quille was a quack. ... But look at me flourishing like a heap of dock leaves you'd vainly strive to smother by covering up with stones, for no man can wither the root or blast the fame of Morgan Quille of Beenahorna. ... Twenty miles to cure a boy with the breast bone down! I would, then, and a hundred miles itself flaking over a side of a country to come at the stiffest case of that disease!

But some of Fitzmaurice's characters, in less formal moments, sound like Boucicault's Conn. A good example occurs in act 1 of *The Waves of the Sea* when Wise James Danagher explains to his family how Rich Danagher inherited land Wise James felt was rightfully his.

And, sez the little old fellow to me, sez he, 'don't mind about Rich's cleverness or his sailing around Yankee Peter, Mr. Danager' sez he, 'for the way he came by the farm was through witchcraft of a three-halfpenny ring he bought from the ugliest divvle you ever see of a black and grey gipsy hag.' ... 'You saw the ring yourself,' sez he, 'and you saw printing inside in it and you didn't know what it was. Two inscriptions, one in Irish and one in French. I don't know what was in French yet,' sez he, 'but I'll tell you after.' 'Don't mind about the French,' sez I, 'but translate for me what was in Irish,' and he did translate it and this was it:

> Who buys this ring buys charms and alarms,
> But the first benefit coming in six bully farms.

Then I understood all—that the virtues was in that ring went through the air, hit something in the brain of Yankee Pete, changing him inside out, with the result that before he gave his last gasp a new will was made and an ignorant understrapper of the White Danaghers became the boss and leading man of the Danagher race.

Curiously, Wise James reverts to slightly more solemn rhetoric toward the end of his speech, backing away from the "sez he," "sez I" recitation.

Conn the Shaughraun is a peasant very much idealized. He is full of spirits (literal and figurative), blarney, and wit. He is a n'er-do-well, but good-natured, full of humor, reckless of danger, inexhaustible in his verbal prowess. Fitzmaurice's true Kerry peasant is no attractive, ebullient Conn the Shaughraun, all play and no work. But the colorful rhetoric is as essential to Mr. Quille and to Teig of the Trees and to Luke Quilter, as it is to Conn. And though Boucicault's Conn and Myles (*The Colleen Bawn*) become models for the eloquent peasant-scoundrel, a big difference between a dramatist like Boucicault and one like Fitzmaurice is that because Boucicault did not see the contradictory tensions in the peasant that Fitzmaurice did, his language does not reflect frustration as well as wild fantasy; his language lacks the heaviness which Fitzmaurice's has—a heaviness necessary to articulate the farcical despair felt by the peasant. The language of Fitzmaurice's dark comedies desecrates any sentimental pieties of an idyllic and pure peasant life which the comic language of Boucicault's irreverent fools set up. And unlike Boucicault's, Fitzmaurice's language is no dream fabric: it is a natural product of colonialism, a Saxon-Celtic hybrid grounded in harsh reality, and not like Boucicault's "Irishese."

In Boucicault's Irish plays, *The Shaughraun, The Colleen Bawn,* and *Arrah-na-Pogue* Conn the Shaughraun, Myles-na-Coppaleen, and Shaun the Post use many stock phrases, yet, for all their Gaelic epithets and thick brogue, they never resort to the "top-of-the-morning" and "broth-of-a-boy" cliches. In the hands of Fitzmaurice a similar but more serious thrust of comic language becomes an ironic weapon which characters wield as their only defense in a world of harsh reality.

There is another music-hall-Boucicaultian turn of language which Fitzmaurice uses often. For example, in *There Are Tragedies and Tragedies* Maura echoes everything her husband Geoffrey says:

GEOFFREY: Dazed, dazed, but not dead.

MAURA: Thank God for that itself, Geoff, that they aren't dead, but dazed.

GEOFFREY: Dazed, dazed but not dead. Not a stir from them. It could be they have completely lost the hearing. And I can see no eye and the way the hat is down on Humphrey and the handkerchief twisted about Kytie.

MAURA: No eye indeed, Geoff and the way the hat is down on Humphrey and the handkerchief twisted about Kytie.

The same thing happens in *The Ointment Blue* between Teig of the Trees and his sidekick brother, Donacha, who repeats key parts of Teig's speeches. These repetitions occur so often in

Boucicault that he may have been the source of Fitzmaurice's own language habit. An example occurs in the last act of *The Shaughraun*. There is a mock wake episode. Conn is stretched out like a corpse, a trick to fool the police and rescue his imprisoned Fenian friend, the rebel Ffoliott. A group of keening neighbors have come to comfort Mrs. O'Kelly:

> CHORUS: Why did ye die?—Why did ye die? Laving us to sigh, och hone! Why did ye die?—Why did ye die? Olaghaun—oh, Olaghaun!
> BIDDY: Oh, oh, oho! Oh, oo, Olaghaun! The widdy had a son—an only son—wail for the widdy!
> CHORUS: Why did ye die?—Why did ye die?
> BIDDY: I see her when she was a fair young girl—a fine young girl, wide a child at her breast.
> CHORUS: Laving us to sigh! Och, hone!
> BIDDY: Then I see a proud woman wid a boy by her side. He was a bould as a bull-calf that runs beside of the cow.
> CHORUS: Why did ye die?—Why did ye die?

From the point of view of Syntax and rhythm, this keen portrays perfectly the Boucicaultian turn of language which Fitzmaurice used so often in his plays, but from another point of view, the example is somewhat unfair, for the phrase "Why did ye die?" is the customary refrain in a keen and not strictly speaking a language trick from Boucicault. However, the dialogue of the mock wake is only one example, though an admirable one; there are others, as:

> FATHER DOLAN: Didn't you give me a promise last Aister—a blessed promise, made on your two knees—that you would lave off dhrink?
> CONN: I did, barrin' one thimbleful a day, just to take the cruelty out o' the wather.
> FATHER DOLAN: One thimbleful. I allowed that concession, no more.
> CONN: God bless ye, ye did; an' I kep' my word.
> FATHER DOLAN: Kept your word! How dare you say that! Didn't I find you ten days after stretched out drunk as a fiddler at Tim O'Malley's wake?

Fitzmaurice's apparent enthusiasm for the rich dialogue of Boucicault's comic rogue-heroes is shared by Synge, O'Casey, and more recently by Brendan Behan. It would not be an exaggeration to say that Irish dramatic language as we know it today had its origins in Boucicault. This Boucicaultian influence only serves to illustrate Fitzmaurice's Irishness, but here again, he is still his own man: he takes what is useful from various sources, but converts this material into something uniquely his own. And he does the same with respect to the Kerry dialect he uses in nearly every play.

VI   Anglo-Irish Dialects

In plays by folk dramatists like Lady Gregory, John Synge, and George Fitzmaurice, language is the first thing we notice. "Let us learn construction from the masters, and dialogue from ourselves."[13] "From ourselves" because in the speech of the Irish peasant there was a vivid and unspoiled language. In this respect the Irish writer enjoyed the advantage of an Elizabethan drawing from the abundant linguistic resources of his time. Dialects spoken in the west and south of Ireland preserve old forms of English. Their history, several centuries old, reveals a syntax and vocabulary partly derived from Irish and partly from Tudor English. Lady Gregory, Synge, and Fitzmaurice had enough Irish to understand its syntax and vocabulary. Synge studied ancient Gaelic under H. d'Arbois de Jubainville and modern Irish in an Aran cottage. In her *Cuchulain of Muirthemne* and *Gods and Fighting Men*, Lady Gregory had executed the most popular translations ever made from the Irish language; before writing a word of her plays, she had filled notebook after notebook with the English of her neighborhood. Furthermore, Synge and Lady Gregory knew Tudor English— Lady Gregory especially, for as Yeats said, "When I knew her first, the *Morte d'Arthur* was her book of books."[14] George Fitzmaurice's father was an Irish speaker, [15] and two of the playwright's sisters, Margaret and Hanora, became fluent speakers. Since George was fourteen when his father died, he did not learn to speak Irish fluently, but he could read it easily and he understood Irish speakers.

Douglas Hyde often wrote of the difficulties encountered in trying to translate Irish into English because the two languages are so different in spirit and idiom. Even so, the English spoken by at least three–quarters of the people of Ireland is largely influenced by Gaelic idioms, for most of those expressions which surprise Americans or Englishmen are really renditions from that Irish which was the language of the speaker's father, grand-father, or great–grandfather.

To give an example, Douglas Hyde tells us in *Beside the Fire*[16] that in his translations he tried to avoid the pluperfect as much as possible, for no such tense exists in Irish, and the people who speak English seem to find no need for it. They will way, "I'd speak sooner if I knew that," where we would say, "if I had know that I would have spoken sooner."

Another prominent feature of Anglo-Irish is its peculiar (to us) use of the verb "to be." In English stress is important, and the meaning of a sentence can be varied according to the stress laid on certain words. But in Gaelic, and therefore Anglo-Irish, the sentence construction emphasizes the meaning, and the most important word comes immediately after the verb "to be." "Is it yourself that is fearing old age?" and "It was my own son hit me." The object may be made prominent: "it's great money and love I've won me in the end of time" or an adverbial addition: "It's soon he'll be coming home." The verb "to be" is used to form tenses and to form moods such as: "Let you be making the beds and cleaning the house." To suggest habit or frequency we get: "would anyone believe the things they do be saying about us?" There is a strong preference for the interrogative form, often to make the affirmative stronger: "and it's that you'd call fun is it, to be abroad in the world with yourself alone?" The effect of these and other related constructions is a series of cadences which make for a pleasing and unified rhythm.

Lady Gregory and John Synge were the first educated man and woman who expressed themselves in the dialect of the people. Boucicault had also used this idiom, but for humorous effects only. He borrowed from any number of dialects, creating in the amalgam a hybrid of what could be called "Irishese," a mongrelized composite that resembles no actual speech, nor is it meant to. Boucicault's purpose was to write dramatic conversa-tions representing how non-Irish, English speakers imagined the Irish spoke. But Lady Gregory and Synge showed that real though idealized peasant idiom could be used to create plays of power and beauty, and they established this Anglo-Irish idiom as the distinctive medium of the Irish drama in the first and most important phase of its development. And it is this idiom which George Fitzmaurice employs so successfully. Plainly, there was a wealth of poetic material here, for the peasant dialect is filled with those devices of language which characterize successful verse drama—highly colored words and complex metaphorical expressions. What would *The Playboy of the Western World* have been without it? Synge acknowledges his debt in the preface to *The Playboy*:

> In writing *The Playboy of the Western World*, as in my other plays, I have used one or two words only that I have not heard among the country people of Ireland, or spoken in my nursery before I could read the newspapers. A certain number of the phrases I employ I have heard also from herds of fishermen along the coast from Kerry to Mayo, or from beggar-women and ballad-singers nearer Dublin; and I am glad to acknowledge how much I owe to the folk imagination of these fine people. Anyone who has lived in real intimacy with the Irish peasantry will know that the mildest sayings and ideas in this play are tame indeed, compared with the fancies one may hear in any little hillside cabin in Geesala, or Carraroe, or Dingle Bay. All art is a collaboration.

Synge, Lady Gregory, and Fitzmaurice, and later O'Casey, achieved the poetic collaboration of art and life by heightening a colloquial language. But their styles are different in many ways for they used different methods and materials. Lady Gregory's dialect, "Kiltartan" as it is called from the name of the district in which Coole stands, lacks Synge's savagery and color, but it has a musical lilt of its own that makes it ideal for comedy. Her plays are models of taut construction, very much influenced by Molière whose plays she translated into "Kiltartan" for performance at the Abbey. The young wife's lament in *The Gaol Gate* is a good example of her classical, economical, precise, neat handling of dialect:

> What way will I be the Sunday, and I going up the hill to Mass? Every woman with her comrade, and Mary Cushin to be walking her love!

> What way will I be the Monday and the neighbours turning their heads from the house? The turf Dennis cut lying on the bog, and no well-wisher to bring it to the hearth!

> What way will I be in the night-time, ,and none but the dog calling after you? Two women to be mixing a cake, and not a man in the house to break it!

> What way will I sow the field, and no man to drive the furrow? The sheaf to be scattered before the spring time that was brought together at the harvest!

Synge's dialect is more luxuriant, more poetic, more memorable. An instance in *The Playboy* is Michael James Flaherty's description, for Christy's benefit, of the funeral he has just attended.

... and wasn't it a shame I didn't bear you along with me to Kate Cassidy's wake, a fine, stout lad, the like of you, for you'd never see the match of it for flows of drink, the way when we sunk her bones at noonday in her narrow grave, there were five men, aye, and six men, stretched out retching speechless on the holy stones. .... And, aren't you a louty schemer to go burying your poor father unbeknownst when you'd a right to throw him on the crupper of a Kerry mule and drive him westwards, like holy Joseph in the days gone by, the way we could have given him a decent burial, and not have him rotting beyond, and not a Christian drinking a smart drop to the glory of his soul?

Fitzmaurice's language is not as carefully wrought as Synge's and it does not have the deliberately measured cadence of Synge's style; yet it has a rhythm and music of its own.

You snake! Is it me have tricks! Is it me! Me to stoop to the dirty ways of the things that do be daubing each other in the puddles and the gutters and the sewers of the world! Me that can sweep them clean in the battlefield of the intellect, making them run like rats fleeping into their dirty holes, or cockroaches racing for their dirty lives before the glint of dawn.[17]

When the day's grand with the sun shining above in the heavens he do be in great mind, and hope and joy do be in him. It's smiling like a half fool he does be to himself and he listening to the thrushes and blackbirds and robineens singing in the little crough below the house, for its your own voice he thinks he hears amongst them and they making ceol [music]. ... But when the day is dull and chilly and the grey rain comes fleeping down, knockroe, he do be lonesome in himself and not a word out of him, he thinking then somehow that your heart is sealed against him and that 'twill never change. ... You'd see him prowling along by the ditches, his head under him and he sighing. And he does be fit to weep itself when he gazes toward Croughderg and no sight of it at all through the drizzle falling on the low bogs.[18]

Fitzmaurice's language is his own Kerry dialect, an odd speech, full of half assimilated alien expressions, submerged proverbs, queer word order. And he did not merely report the exuberant

Kerry idiom; he magnified it and increased its tempo and vigor. Like Synge, he incorporated many phrases he had heard, but his language is no more a literal transcription of actual speech that Synge's was. Austin Clarke has said that Fitzmaurice's dialect seems to catch its pace from the fantastically long place names one finds in Kerry.

In the preface to *The Playboy of the Western World* Synge said:

When I was writing "The Shadow of the Glen," some years ago, I got more aid than any learning could have given me from a chink in the floor of the old Wicklow house where I was staying, that let me hear what was being said by the servant girls in the kitchen. This matter, I think, is of importance for in countries where the imagination of the people, and the language they use, is rich and living, it is possible for a writer to be rich and copious in his words, and at the same time to give the reality, which is the root of all poetry, in a comprehensive and natural form.

Fitzmaurice went even further, saying "sure anybody who could write down the sayings of Kerry people could fool anyone he was a poet."[19] There was indeed, as Yeats said, a wealth of poetic material available for the taking. That however, is part of the story: the other part is artistic selection and creation which brings a "natural" line to life. Synge, Lady Gregory, and Fitzmaurice put these peasant down on paper, and made them think and talk in the language they customarily used. But the language the dramatists created had style. All language begins with speech but when it develops to the point of becoming a literary medium, it only seems like speech. Synge's dialogue, for example, so easy to read, cost him an infinity of pains, and each play went through many drafts.

Fitzmaurice's use of distinctive language within the general pattern of Anglo-Irish speech is certainly one of his chief characteristics. Ernest A. Boyd was the first critic to recognize this:

The "joyless and pallid words," which Synge condemned, find no place in what Fitzmaurice has written, though he uses no expression traceable to any of his predecessors. The Anglo-Irish idiom as he employs it offers no analogies either with Hyde and Synge or Lady Gregory, beyond the fact of their common source in Gaelic which, if not the potent instrument of Synge, is measurably finer than the monotonous 'Kiltartanese' and its minor variants, in vogue with the later playwrights. George Fitzmaurice has, therefore, imagination and style of a sufficiently personal quality to give him rank as the greatest folk dramatist since the death of J. M. Synge.[20]

The Anglo-Irish idiom employed by Fitzmaurice is closer to that used by Synge than it is to that used by Lady Gregory. Of Synge's plays *The Playboy of the Western World* offers the closest parallel. Although the play is set in Mayo, much of the language in *The Playboy* came from visits Synge made to the Irish speaking sections of Kerry.

The plays of Synge and Lady Gregory are often described as "dialect," but their language does not present much difficulty to anyone reasonably conversant with standard English. There are not many unfamiliar words; it is rather a question of construction and usage. This cannot be said of George Fitzmaurice. Words derived directly from Gaelic are not found so commonly in the plays of other folk playwrights as they are in the plays of Fitzmaurice. Fitzmaurice listened carefully to those about him who spoke a language which was an unusual combination of common English and Gaelic words in an area where Gaelic was slowly giving way to English.

When the *Dramatic Fantasies* was published in 1967, various reviewers commented on Fitzmaurice's language. An anonymous contributor to *Choice* observed that "Writing at a time when delight in folklore and idiomatic language was both genuine and formative, Fitzmaurice had a remarkable ear for dialect literature."[21]

Another reviewer wrote:

This is the first of three volumes of the work of a forgotten dramatist from the Irish Literary Renaissance. . . . The publishers hope to prompt an interest in having the plays performed. Unfortunately, the dialogue is so heavy a brogue that performance is almost inconceivable. We would need one of the magic talismans which appear in each of the fantasies to tackle lines like, "still, 'tis meself is thinking 'tis a reckless thing to be hysing this Mr. Quille on a false pretense that Jaymony has his breast bone down.[22]

Even Austin Clarke, who greatly admires George Fitzmaurice, has said: "The hardy language of Fitzmaurice should survive the turn of fashion for it is his own but I feel that it would be improved for us if some of the strained grammar and idiom of the period were discreetly excised."[23] At the end of *The Dramatic Fantasies* which he edited, Clarke lists some Irish words (though he ignores far too many) frequently used in the plays—words like agragil, geasa, plamaus, sheefra, tasby. Howard Slaughter in *George Fitzmaurice and his Enchanted Land* has compiled a more complete list (181 words) based on the many Irish words used in the nonfantasies. He also has located and listed fifty-two place-names used in these plays. It is apparent that Fitzmaurice attempted to reproduce a language closer to the Gaelic original than that produced by either Lady Gregory or Synge. Joseph Holloway corroborates this in his diary entry on October 3, 1907:

The comedy [*The Country Dressmaker*] was not long on its way when it was easy to see that Fitzmaurice had a grip on his subject and that his dialogue was the real article and his men and women those one might meet any day down in Kerry. Two natives from Kerry sat before me and assured me that the turn of phrase of the Kerry people was aptly copied, and that the types were perfect specimens of the ordinary folk to be met with down there. 'Even the very names of the characters are Kerry to the backbone.' This opinion from those on the spot, as it were, was very flattering to the dramatist; and, as he clothed the simple story . . . with humour and tenderness in easy, natural dialogue, he won over the audience completely and romped home a successful dramatic writer.[24]

Decades later, Michael O'Connor, a member of the Listowel Players, told Colonel Fitzmaurice that only Kerry-born actors could successfully play his cousin's dramas because only they spoke his language.

It is true that Fitzmaurice uses far too many Gaelic words to suit an Englishman or an American, and this, more than anything else, probably accounts for his obscurity. And yet, when Fitzmaurice breaks away from the language of Kerry, his plays fail. In *The Coming of Ewn Andzale* and in *One Evening Gleam*, Fitzmaurice abandons the Kerry dialect with the result that the dialogue is not convincing. These are the only two plays Fitzmaurice set in Dublin.

The dialogue of *One Evening Gleam* is much superior to that of *The Coming Ewn Andzale*, but it is not the racy Dublinese of Sean O'Casey. Actually, Mrs. Cleary's and Mrs. Hannigan's conversation, which forms the greater art of *One Evening Gleam*, is natural and lifelike, but not memorable. On these two occasions when Fitzmaurice departs from the Kerry idiom, his language becomes artificial. This is surprising when one considers that Fitzmaurice spent his entire adult life in Dublin. And yet for a man who lived so long in Dublin, surely the language must have been his. At any rate he must have stored up a rich word-hoard during his first twenty years in Kerry, and most of the time he was able to draw upon his memory and imaination.

The reason these plays are not as exciting as say, the fantasies, is that Fitzmaurice was trying to be as realistic as possible. Yeats' chief objection to realistic plays was realistic language.

After all, is not the greatest play, not the play that gives the sensation of an external reality, but the play in which there is the greatest abundance of life itself, of the reality that is in our minds? Is it possible to make a work of art, which needs every subtlety of expression if it is to reveal what hides itself continually, out of a dying, or at any rate a very ailing language? And all language but that of the poets and of the poor is already bedridden. We have, indeed, persiflage, the only speech of educated men that expresses a deliberate enjoyment of words; but persiflage is not a true language. It is impersonal; it is not in the midst but on the edge of life; it covers more character than it discovers.[25]

When Captain James Davenport in *The Coming of Ewn Andzale* speaks, it is persiflage; and it is very silly besides. "You should make allowances, my boy, for what we used to call in my young days a blue stocking. Then of course she is getting near thirty and no proposals. She is three years older than Cissie, isn't she?" Obviously Fitzmaurice means to portray the wordiness and pomposity of the captain, but Fitzmaurice's own excesses create an overall effect of fatuousness, as for example when the captain asks about his own two daughters—"she is three years older than Cissie, isn't she?" As stilted as Captain Davenport can be, no one is any better. Queenie, his daughter is a good deal worse; her talk is not only overly formal, it is pompous:

No wonder about it, but if your mental balance had been stronger the worry would not have caused such a brainstorm resulting in the bizarre development of your writing a letter to yourself. Otherwise you would probably have effected an endo-psychic transfer, that is you would have driven the trouble from your brain down into your breadbasket, with, very likely, nothing more serious accruing there from than a severe, but temporary, attack of gastritis.

The speech is in character, for Queenie is overbearing, but it exhibits a fault in Fitzmaurice's writing; moreover, it is too stiff and pretentious. Her father's reply is equally stilted. "I have already told you, Queenie, that I have never heard such nonsense in my life before as that I have been hearing from you today and now I tell it to you again. Even if Ewn Andzale doesn't turn up tonight, that wouldn't prove that your mother, Mrs. Davenport, did such an outlandish and nonsensical thing as to write a letter to herself."

Even without the rather unnecessary identification of her mother as Mrs. Davenport, the speech is dull. And so it goes throughout the entire play, with nothing to redeem it. For an author dealing with dull and supercilious people, there is always the danger that he too will become boring and pompous. Of course some writers deliberately match content and form in this way, but in Fitzmaurice's *The Coming of Ewn Andzale* this does not seem to be the case. The language of *One Evening Gleam* while not poetic is natural. Obviously Fitzmaurice could not write of a higher class as well as he could depict tenement dwellers. The more he tries to mold genteel language, the more stilted it becomes. The fact that this is Fitzmaurice at his most ineffectual, shows how important language is to a Fitzmaurice play. For Fitzmaurice had a real flair for dialogue, though it seems to have abandoned him here. The language in this play is awful throughout. It is totally unpoetic and completely unlifelike. It is not even good persiflage. Queenie is not only the biggest show-off with respect to her language, she is also thoroughly nasty. She says to her mother:

Oh, you did more than what I would call a share of them, Mama. You bought the Times and the Daily Telegraph for the sole purpose of doing their crosswords, also the Sunday Times and the Observer, not to mention the books of crosswords you went through. You didn't content yourself with the simpler ones either, and but for its pathetic aspect it would have been diverting considering your educational background, such as your indifferent grounding in the Classics and your lack of a thorough knowledge of Greek and Roman mythology, your continued and desperate but invariably unavailing attempts to solve the Ximenes Crossword in the Observer. And it was whilst reflecting on Mama's crossword activities that I got on the explanation of that nondescript cognomen, Ewn Andzale.

This is artificial language, not living speech. It is a case of the self-conscious stylist, both character and author, showing off. Aeneas Canty and Teig of the Trees, and even Roche and Gunn show off too, but nowhere is their pretense so unappealing as here. Besides, we know Fitzmaurice is making fun of characters like Aeneas and Teig, but with the Davenports, despite their English name, the obviously intended ridicule does not come off. This play is completely uncharacteristic of Fitzmaurice.

It has been said, reproachfully, that dialect laanguage, like Synge's Wicklow and Fitzmaurice's Kerry was impossible to copy and fatally easy to parody. But today especially, when much serious drama either consists of "pallid and joyless words" or is downright inarticulate, there is a joy and delight to be found in these plays with their flow of language.

VII *Imagery*

Artistic transformation makes Synge's and Fitzmaurice's language distinct from the actual language spoken by the peasants as each is distinct from the other. For Synge it is mainly the world of nature that he idealizes in his imagery. His primitive characters are instinctively a part of nature and in awe of its grandeur and mystery. Even in *The Playboy of the Western World* where the main tension is created by Christy's imagination which transforms his dream to be somebody into actuality, there is a great deal of nature imagery. All of Synge's images are clearly derived from common experience and none is inappropriate to the simplicity of the peasants.

And like Synge, Fitzmaurice uses an imagery grounded in simple everyday life. But when Fitzmaurice's imagery is closely examined, it is seen to be sparse, simple, and rather unimaginative. Phrases containing unexciting images like "sound as a black oak," "healthy as a crow," "sound as bell-metal," "night as black as pitch," "as grey as the hills," "quiet and obedient as a tame duck," "hardy as a jacksnipe" abound. And there are many more along these same lines: "Say but the word, Captain, and, by Jaycus, there's cake made of his skull";[26] "The grass will be growing to your doorstep before I come back to you";[27] "Tis true she got the happiest death—the happiest death I ever seen. Like the candle she went, and it shoving near the break of day";[28] "Big people do have friends and get many chances. When a big fellow goes down unless he's a harum-scarum altogether he'll be up again in a week's time as gay as a bee for himself. Big people are like corks. . . . Small people are like lead, once they go down with them for ever more and per omnia saecula saeculorum."[29]   This kind of imagery is merely illustrative; anyone could think of such images. But for Synge it is by means of the image that we grasp his uniquely fresh vision of things. His images shift rapidly and say much. Synge uses the same homely verbal texture Fitzmaurice does, but includes a comparison, often startling, between objects which are apparently dissimilar in images like: "his chin the way it would take the bark from the edge of an oak board you'd have a building a door"; "if the mitred bishops seen you that time, they'd be the like of the holy prophets, I'm thinking, do be straining the bars of Paradise to lay eyes on the Lady Helen of Troy, and she abroad, pacing back and forward, with a nosegay in her garden shawl"; "crossing the hills when the fog is on them, the time the little stick would seem as big as your arm, and a rabbit as big as a bay horse, and a stack of turf as big as a towering church in the city of Dublin"; "she after going by with her head turned the way you'd see a priest going where there'd be a drunken man in the side ditch talking with a girl"; "that whitish yellowy hair she has does be soon turning the like of a handful of thin grass you'd see rotting, where the wet lies, at the north end of a sty." Synge groups similies; Fitzmaurice does not. Synge particularizes a conventional image and makes it fresh; generally Fitzmaurice cannot. The poetry of Synge's dialect is just that much greater than Fitzmaurice's because of its "metaphysical" hyperbole and the degree to which it is made specific by apt, tangible, and immediate associations.

Is this to say, then, that Fitzmaurice is a good writer of Irish dialect, but essentially a weak imitator of Synge? No, decidedly not. It is obvious Fitzmaurice was greatly influenced by Synge. His best images are typically Synge-like:

Didn't I pronounce it and indeed it wouldn't be easy to mistake the cut of that high-diddle warrant and the way the big fellow is steering himself making for this cabin putting one leg out and the other after, like a pensioned peeler, throwing the chest and shaping.[30]

The next evening the pub was packed, but the half-gent made no effort to give me, aged or not, a chance to get near the counter. And indeed 'tisn't alone him but the whole issue would not shift the one-thirtieth part of an inch even to facilitate the Almighty God himself if he came down from heaven and his throat cracking for a pint.[31]

No tears I'm saying but be bold in hearing it: a queer change will be seen in the moon, hailstones in the shape of black goose-eggs will come rattling on the slates. A crackling will be heard in Ireland and through the known world itself, if it should happen that great Diarmuid Rue Mullarkey goes down.[32]

Praying for him myself should be, but the words would stick in my gullet the way I am tormented from every abuse of the world whirled about like an old bruised and battered tin-can. But 'tis for the crimes of more I am punished, Eileen, for it's nothing I ever done out of the way to deserve these stripes uncommon and severe, scarified all my days with troubles walloping at me as fierce as hailstones flamming on the slate. But now the pinnacle of my miseries is reached at last in this grief about Eugene, and the heart and soul is kilt in me entirely.[33]

The cadences and rhythms and images above are somewhat closer to Synge's than much of the rest of Fitzmaurice's writing. However, Fitzmaurice repeats his images a great deal, something Synge never does. In the examples above, the image of hailstones on slate is used twice. Fitzmaurice is guilty of this repetition in imagery again and again throughout the plays, suggesting an imagination not as fecund as Synge's.

In Fitzmaurice's defense, it is not easy to imitate him, while Synge, was followed by a number of imitators of little ability—so many in fact, that Gerald MacNamara parodied in all in *The Mist That Does Be On the Bog*. Fitzmaurice's language shows that his vision is not like Synge's; his images are not so memorable and he does not arrange metaphors like Synge. But he is first and foremost a master of dialogue writing. He can make his characters say great things at high moments.

VIII *Dialogue*

The dialogue of *The Moonlighter*, for example, is consistently bold, hard, imaginative. Big William Cantillon's land grabbing

speech in act 3 vividly and luxuriantly personifies the intoxica-
tion for property that overpowers a landgrabber. The language
throughout the play is inventive, not only serving to sketch in the
more violent and harsh characters directly, but by its incongruity
to make us compassionate with gentler souls. For instance, when
Malachi discovers Eugene's unfired gun, Ellen expresses her joy
that her son could not have killed his uncle, Big William
Cantillon, but in a speech containing some phrases startingly
inappropriate to the relief she feels.

Ah, my heart is bubbling at the sight of that woeful engine, rusted and
ruined and innocent of the precious blood of man!—My heart is
bubbling. We are in the heel of our days, and it must be the Lord in his
mercy is thinking of relenting towards us and lifting from us the heavy
hand that kept our noses to the ground and broke the melt in us so long.
Flaming years have passed over our heads, and we have brought our
scars out of the raging battling times, but there is a quietness all around,
and now at last, maybe, there is in my bosom the warmest hope we'll all
rise contented at tomorrow's dawn, calm and rational for ourselves,
without the pains of villainous torments darting through our eyeballs,
and we blinking out at the sky of heaven and the fields so green.

Though the speech is ironical (Ellen is about to lose her
husband), Fitzmaurice evokes great sympathy for her by the
effective seriocomic mood of her utterances. Speeches like
these, with their stylized cadence, imagery, and selection of
heightened details, are something quite different from a
collection of colloquial phrases, for Fitzmaurice embroidered his
Kerry dialect into inimitable dialogue, like the opening of *The
Magic Glasses*, for example:

MAINEEN: See now, Padden, all is in readiness for Mr. Quille, let him
come what hour 'twill match him. And, oh hierna! the heart is rising in
me at the thought of his putting Jaymony off that habit of going up in
the top loft, our fine sons, Roger and Frynk, lighting with shame on
account of it, and saying they'll come home to us no more on their
holydays if their brother don't get shut of his canter.
PADDEN: Still, 'tis meself is thinking tis a reckless thing to be hysing
this Mr. Quille on a false pretense that Jaymony has his breast bone
down [stiff shoulder] 'Tis unknown what the stranger will do when
he'll know the truth, he an almighty passionate man, they do be saying,
that don't like to be deceived. ... Faith, from what I'm after hearing
'twill take pains to please him, whatever way you take him. And 'tisn't
alone having the punch steaming on the table to him almost he's over
the threshold will do; for Mary Sofine says the half-sovereign must be

slipped to him unbeknownst, the pride is that big in him. To put all words into one, Maineen, the notions and capers of the devil is in this Mr. Quille.

MAINEEN: 'Tis the same with all them geniuses. Padden, every mother's son of them nothing but notions and capers since the world began itself.

PADDEN: But maybe he isn't the big genius we thought him after all. Sure, some say 'twas great fame he got the first day from curing the breast bone down made people go running to him with this and that in the line of diseases, and, the pride and gumption rising in him, he couldn't renayge himself attempting all before him—things he was dull of as before him—things he was dull of as the biggest fool walking the road.

MAINEEN: Glory! Listen to that, and yourself has biggest praiser—drawing down but a few nights ago itself how he cured Mary Canty of the dropsies and the swellings with his dilution of the white heather that does be growing in the bogs.

This is an illustration of a dialogue style in which the conception of the characters as well as the language is magnified in such a way that Fitzmaurice allows the characters to expose and enjoy their sublime folly. He uses this kind of rhetoric for most of his comic characters when they are stimulated or provoked, which is most of the time—characters like Quille, Quilter, Teig, John Daly and Jim.

The most noticeable quality of Fitzmaurice's dialogue is that so many plays open with a concise, dramatic disclosure of what is to come. His opening dialogue conveys to the audience everything by seeming to tell it nothing—by letting it catch up with the characters as it sees them actually living and overhears their talk to each other—like the following from *The Dandy Dolls*:

GREY MAN: God bless you, lady. *(pause)* God bless, honest woman! *(pause)* Sour female, it's God bless I'm saying!

CAUTH: Oh, God bless! But if it's alms you're wanting, Grey fellow, I'm thinking you're come to the wrong shop. For there isn't meal in the house, nor spuds in the house but the red raw starvation, as might be plain to you by the cut of that ashy creature sitting there on the hob with the map of the world painted on his burnt spangled shins.

GREY MAN: God bless the child, I say! But it's no alms I come for, woman dear, or no reception in the line of lodging or of food. Indeed, it's himself I'm wanting, your darling husband, Mr. Roger Carmody; and is himself at home?

CAUTH: Himself is at home, but I'm thinking he's engaged.

GREY MAN: *(With long intonation)* Engaged! What sort of talk is that in a cabin black with soot? Engaged! Sure a man could be engaged and could spare a little time.

CAUTH: He could if he wasn't my man, that has time and play-time and whips of time again, but still for want of time is in such a devil's own fix that he can't renayge himself to put a sop in the thatch, fix a hoop in that leaking oven, or settle a pot-hooks on which to hang the pot. He don't earn as much as a shilling in the week, and all the same he's engaged, sir, and always engaged is he.

GREY MAN: That's like a riddle you'd hear from a child—I went to the wood and I picked a thorn, riddle-me riddle-me-ree.

CAUTH: *(Sourly)* A sore subject I'd be riddling on, then, that booby man of mine; for may the devil fly away with the day he drew on him that practice of making dandy dolls. Isn't he well engaged, glory be to God?

Good dialogue, especially at the opening of a play, reveals and explains. Nearly every Fitzmaurice play opens this way. Because of this gift for writing dialogue, we can think of Fitzmaurice as a born playwright because reality, or that part of reality he sees, can be compressed into dialogue and expressed by it.

Fitzmaurice is a writer who lived among and understood a people who shared a common idiom and common experiences, and in this he discovered the roots of a unique and potentially poetic language. The way of life and the imagination of these Kerry people did give him an initial advantage over many twentieth-century dramatists because it enabled him to write about a reality, admittedly limited, with some poetic richness and depth. Even so, although the idiom of the Kerry peasants was unusually vivid, it still had to be shaped into apt dramatic diction. Firzmaurice did not just collect words and images and string them together. He made a selection from the Kerry idiom and thereby created language which was authentic but certainly more compressed and luxurious than the actual speech of a Kerryman. And of course this is precisely what Synge did with the Wicklow dialect and Lady Gregory with the Kiltartan. They all three developed, heightened, and intensified what was already more animated than the average.

IX   Setting

The base of George Fitzmaurice's personal theater was Kerry, where by means of restricted dialect and characterization he expressed his seriocomic vision. Of course there are many plays by dramatists other than Fitzmaurice which are set in Kerry, but for Fitzmaurice almost every play he wrote is located in Kerry, and in a very specific part of North Kerry. Growing up in this region gave Fitzmaurice a keen sense of the peasants' plight. There is no idealization whatever in his portrayal of the economic and social conditions of the locale, nor of its marital customs and its local superstitions, nor is there any hedging in his depiction of the people's insularity. And what is most characteristic about Fitzmaurice's use of these settings is the way he merges realistic "local color" with fantasy, but a fantasy that is appropriate to the settings. How does Fitzmaurice make his settings function this way? First of all, he puts the places he grew up in into his plays.

Fitzmaurice was born near Listowel, North Kerry. Though a Kerryman, he was not from the popular tourist region of the south, but from the little visited north, in the area of the Stacks Mountains. He grew up in Duagh, a village on the River Feale. Duagh is about five miles upstream from Listowel and four from Abbeyfeale, which lies just over the river in Country Limerick. The Feale creates a lovely valley. It is a land of abrupt mountains and dark glens, of scattered woods and small blue lakes, a land which still holds a remnant of the ancient Gaelic civilization. The roads of Duagh, for example, have not changed for hundreds of years; they are bordered by hedges entwined with furze or by strong, dry-stone walls. It is in these mountains and glens of North Kerry that most of the plays take place. The names of its villages, farms, and mountains abound in his plays.

In *The Ointment Blue*, for example, the action takes place in the "Kingdom of Carraweira," the Barna country which lies in North Kerry and West Limerick, but the specific locale is near "sweet Duagh" as Proud Aeneas describes it. The village where Fitzmaurice actually grew up is described here and in *The Toothache*. In *The Toothache* Duagh is not called by name but Jim gives the following description of the locale: "And, is it to view life you skelped down here to this capital village of our parish,—a little town with the population near a hundred, five public houses and the Great House within the one fourth of a mile of it itself." This description gives a fairly good picture of Fitzmaurice's hometown, Duagh, and the "Great House" which is so very important to the action of *The Moonlighter* is probably Duagh House, the Fitzmaurice ancestral home.

In nearly every play there are specific references to towns in the Duagh area. The *Pie-Dish* is laid in North Kerry. Old Leum is very eager to show his completed pie-dish to his three remaining friends, Old Moll of Carraweira, a town just across the River Feale from Duagh, Teigue of Scartaglen, a village near Castle Island in Kerry, and Jack Bui of Meenscubawn, a town between Duagh and Abbeyfeale. Leum's daughter, Johanna, complains about tramping all day from Glounasroan, a town about a mile from Abbeyfeale. The priest grumbles about having to administer the last sacrament to Leum when he had urgent business in Lyre, a village about nine miles south of Duagh. In *The Moonlighter* many of the same places are specified: Lyre; Gloutaine a town nearby; Derk, a hill three miles south of Duagh; and so on. In *The Terrible Baisht* the action takes place outside a public house on the afternoon of a big fair day in the town of Barravale, a fictitious name. But the play does not proceed very far before Mount Eagle is spoken of, another town near Duagh.

Innumerable examples could be cited, but such a cataloging of Kerry place-names used in the plays would give the impression that Fitzmaurice did nothing more with his settings than mention place names, when, in fact, he did much more. Nowhere but in Kerry could the action of most of the plays have taken place; there is a pervasive reflection of its historical and social conditions. *The Country Dressmaker*, for example, is a story of Kerry matchmaking. *The Moonlighter* concerns the cooled ardor of an old Fenian; it is a play about the agrarian revolution of the 1880s, as it happened in Kerry. Actually North Kerry has a certain importance in Irish history, and this is mirrored in many plays. A Fitzmaurice was the first lord of Kerry, and George claims a five-hundred-year descent from the fifth lord. In the sixteenth century, Gerald Fitzgerald, fifteenth earl of Desmond and heir to nearly all of Munster (County Kerry is in the province of Munster), married his widowed cousin, the countess of Ormond, a member of another powerful family. Before Queen Elizabeth could hope for profits from her Irish colony, certain affairs had to be put in order, not the least of which was pacifying the huge province of Munster, and so

Gerald who through marriage had effected the merger of two influential Munster families, was summoned to England in 1562 to confer with the queen. Three years later he was called to England again, this time because Elizabeth wanted to settle a dispute between him and his stepson, Thomas, earl of Ormond. Ormond, a Protestant and a favorite with Elizabeth was soon at liberty to return to Ireland, while Gerald was confined in England for years. He was finally allowed to leave in 1573 only after giving up much land as a ransom. In the meantime, a cousin, Captain James Fitzmaurice Fitzgerald rallied men in his support and instituted rebellions in Munster. It was this Fitzmaurice who sought help against the English from Philip II of Spain. In 1579 Fitzmaurice did get a few soldiers and many promises from Philip. He was killed a short time later in a skirmish in Limerick. Finally in 1583 Gerald was killed and the Munster rebellions were over. Fitzmaurice's keen awareness of all this is evident throughout the plays. None of this distinguished background was really much help to him, but there is something very appropriate in it for a man who was concerned with the specifically Irish problem of the disparaged, disinherited, and alienated artist.

Fitzmaurice's work is a direct result of Kerry folktales, speech, and everyday life (almost every play is set in a farmer's kitchen). Over and over again we see peasant mores alluded to: the obligations of the child to his parents, for example. In *The Country Dressmaker* and *The Pie-Dish* the child is responsible for the parent. Almost all of the characters are equal to one another: they are nearly all country farmers, the chief occupation of rural Ireland. The rural obsession with improving the land emerges often, as well as the fact that few farmers really know what they are doing. Luke Dennehy's refusal (*The Terrible Baisht*) to read pamphlet 156 ("Don't read any more of it. It might be a big important looking envelope but there is nothing in it but bosh"), and his resultant monetary loss typify the total lack of communication between Irish bureaucracy and the peasant. And who would know better than George Fitzmaurice who worked all his life for the Agricultural and Congested District Boards. The gombeen man (moneylender) has more influence in a small town than any government official.

Over and over again Fitzmaurice portrays small town suspicion of anyone even slightly different, of the man or women from a distant place. In *The Terrible Baisht* John Daly is referred to by the Kerry butcher, Shannessy, as "a stranger to us from an outlandish place that's neither Limerick nor Kerry, and in its own Country Cork is beyond the corn line, a woebegone no man's land of a spot notwithstanding its being only ten miles or so away, is as foreign as Kamskatchka to the natives of this town." Similarly in *The Simple Hanrahans* Daisy the barmaid thinks of the Hanrahans as everyone else does: "What harm but the Simple Hanrahans being almost furriners as I might say — why it's only three years since they bought the farm they have settled on here after coming from County Cork."

Fitzmaurice has presented the Kerry peasant to us as he is and as he sees himself. *The Enchanted Land* and *The Ointment Blue* are so very delightful precisely because they set forth royalty as the folk might see them. Part of the fun comes from the fact that the peasants themselves are putting on a show of being something other than what they are. The procession of King Conacher and his queen throughout the farm lands is entertaining because ordinarily one thinks of a royal procession in a city for the benefit of crowds of people. Aeneas' airs are peasant pretenses: it is a universal fact of life in small towns when people have minor roles they get very officious. And the Irish peasant's love of exaggeration and redundance is shown over and over again.

Isn't it me screeched the good news to Jane Quinlan, the boolumshee [a boaster] that will spread the good news over the known world.[34]

. . . we the fooleens neglecting house and home tearing through the world after him.[35]

The complications are excruciating and are scarifying me. Overwhelmed as they are now with dazzlement and stupidity how are we to convince them that it took six weeks for us that are only two miles away to hear of a tragedy the reports of which of a certainty were flashing through Europe and Amerikay, through continents and islands, to Pittsburgh and San Francisco, and if said it, to the distant realms of Japan, formerly called Cathay.[36]

Significantly when Fitzmaurice abandons Kerry, as he does in only two plays, *One Evening Gleam* and *The Coming of Ewn Andzale*, he succeeds only moderately in one and fails miserably in the other.

The Coming of Ewn Andzale is total disappointment. The strong character and vivid personality of the Kerry peasant is missing in the very unattractive Davenport family. The family lives in Monkstown, a suburb of Dublin on the Irish Sea. Perhaps the failure is owing to the fact Fitzmaurice knew nothing of the middle-class family desperately wanting to "get on" in the world.

One Evening Gleam is set in the heart of Dublin—south of the Liffey River and about one-half mile southwest of St. Stephen's Green. The whole action, consisting of the reminiscings of three women, takes place in Mrs. Cleary's apartment in a tenement house in Great Longford Street. There are references to pubs, suburbs, parks, bridges, places of entertainment which did or do exist in Dublin. Fitzmaurice lived all his adult life in Dublin, so we see what he loved about the city in this play. As Mrs. Clearly and Mrs. Hannigan and Phoebe Tollemache talk, the Dublin of fifty years ago reveals itself.

There wasn't a week but we would go either to the Tivoli or the Empire and we went to places that th' ould parson's daughter never saw, in our earlier married days, adventuring into funny places like the Mechanics where the Abbey Theatre is now and to Pat Kinsella's at the back of Jammet's, where the ticket was fourpence but you'd get a big mayjum bottle of stout for half the ticket when you got in. . . .

Moreover there is pub crawling with the gay Mrs. Hannigan and visits into secret snugs with Phoebe Tollemache in taverns like the Cat and Canary, the Ivy House, or Baggot's in the park.

Quaintness is not part of Fitzmaurice's "Dublinese," nor is his urban speech filled with the strident rhythms and speech patterns of Kerry speech. But the same provincial mistrust of anyone different, characteristic of lower–class people, whether of Kerry farmers or of Dublin tenement dwellers, is depicted in *One Evening Gleam*. Nancy Hannigan tells Mrs. Cleary that the reason the old bachelor, who is "prodestant," and who lives in their tenement, does not take any notice of Phoebe, is "th' ould batchelor was jilted in his young days. He's a Corkman and they say they never forgive a thing like that down in that part of the world."

Fitzmaurice instinctively understood the peasant mind. He dramatized what Lady Gregory came to realize about the poor folk of rural Ireland when she began her search for folk tales among the country people.

As I listened, I was moved by the strange contrast between the poverty of the tellers and the splendours of the tales. These men who failed in life, and were old and withered, or sickly, or crippled, had not laid up dreams of good houses and fields and sheep and cattle; for they had never possessed enough to think of the possession of more as a possibility. It seemed as if their lives had been so poor and rigid in circumstance that they did not fix their minds, as more prosperous people might do, on thoughts of customary pleasure."[37]

According to Lady Gregory, "The stories that they love are of quite visionary things . . . " of underwater habitations, of "brown women" who seduce by magic, of the Land of Mananaan, of the twelve-toed irrepressible Elaine who becomes queen of Ireland by means of a magic ball of yarn, of incredibly obtuse kings and courtiers, of Protestant bishops afraid of boozy priests, of mermaids, of linnaun shees, of princesses who must depend on rich Texas uncles, of hags, beautiful or withered, depending on the view of the beholder. Fitzmaurice dramatized these stories the peasant loved, and he set them always in Kerry. Very often in the fantasies, we are simultaneously in Tir-na-n-ogue[38] and in North Kerry. *The Dandy Dolls* with its fearful grey man of Doon and its swooping Hag of Barna places us in an unreal wonderland. Yet there is an isle of Doon; it is an island in the Shannon Estuary near Ballybunnion. How real is a hag who can carry Roger Carmody away to her den in the Barna hills? Barna is an actual place: a summit in Country Limerick. It is significant that the hag is not from Kerry; her "foreign-ness" makes her all the more frightening. *The Linnaun Shee* is about a fairy and her spells of magic. She seduces her very willing victims around Toor, a town three miles southeast of Duagh, and around Glounaneinta, a town near Castle Island, Kerry, and around Bungleshen, a town three miles south of Duagh. The Linnaun Shee herself chants:

> Come away, come along, come away—
> Come and we'll go roaming;
> Fast by the winding Feale we'll rove.

The Feale is the river on which Duagh is located.

In *The Waves of the Sea* Wise James Danagher is from Scartaglen, a village near Castle Island, Kerry. Significantly, again, a non-Kerry place in mentioned: the White Danaghers, the poor branch of the family, had migrated, years before the play opens, to the North of Cork. The Red Danaghers are the

most powerful family between the Feale and the Geale and
between the Geale and the ocean. The Geale River flows into
the Feale at Listowel. And Dhoul-na-Ferris is a fairy-tale name
for an actual island in the Bay of Doon. This surface confusion of
the real Kerry evoking a never-never land is only fitting for a
man whose flights of imaginative fantasy were firmly grounded
in a stoic acceptance of human nature. The early Yeats and the
changeless AE tried to feed the Irish on fairy cottoncandy and to
lead them to the Land of Heart's Desire. But never Fitzmaurice.
His Kerry is the real article with real peasants in spite of his use
of fantastic locales.

Basically Fitzmaurice's work owes little to anyone except the
Kerry people, the "wicked old children" as he called them. He
went his own private way, fashioning strange little dramas from
the raw material of Kerry peasant life. He was writing about the
most remote and primitive part of Ireland (The Blasket Islands,
not inhabited, are in Kerry and are the westernmost portion of
Europe). The constantly changing light and weather are
unnerving. One guidebook warns that the mountains in Kerry are
not to be trifled with when the mists come down. To this day the
people are haunted by tales of sea monsters, mermaids, and
sharks. This is why in *The Green Stone* Martineen Collopy's
family, trying to rise in the world, are embarassed by his silly
antics with his green stone given him by a mermaid. Even though
they desperately want to get rid of the hated object and get
Martineen to work like any other respectable farmer, deep down
they fear retaliatory consequences from the mermaid.

Isn't it from a mermaid he got the green stone down by the sayshore the
time he was a garsoon. They do be saying she has no legs, but if she
hasn't itself, I hear she can catch hold of her tail and rowling over the
land like sixty, and hop and bump like a football over ditches and
hedges and all; and maybe 'tis into you she'd rowl and give a shlap of
her tail you wouldn't be the better of during the dear days of your life,
if it isn't to gobble you up she would, or hyse you down to the say she
might itself.

Yeats corroborates such superstitions: "'Do the fishermen along
here know anything about the mermaids?' I asked a woman of a
village in Country Dublin. 'Indeed, they don't like to see them at
all,' she answered 'for they always bring bad weather.'"[39]

The Kerry villages are haunted by Irish chiefs, fairies, and

Spaniards. The Grey Men of Doon are "bauble makers to the King and Queen of Spain." Mention of Spain turns up again and again throughout the plays. Why Spain? Probably because after the Reformation, and more so after the marriage of Queen Mary and Philip II, cordial but secret relations had been maintained between Spain and Ireland. In 1571 Queen Elizabeth's deputy complained in a letter that Ireland was overrun with "Spanish spies and vermin."[40] Moreover Dingle (in south Kerry) became a major port and developed a lively trade with Spain until England's defeat of the Armada in 1588 ended Spanish and Irish ties.

What one gets, then, from Fitzmaurice, is the specifically Kerry experience. Daisy describes the simple Hanrahans "with their beards and pipes and all aren't they like little old children, glory be to God." She is really describing the Kerry peasant as Fitzmaurice saw him. To everyone's surprise, the Hanrahans are not simple, and neither, Fitzmaurice is saying, are the Kerry peasants. His plays are not a surface photograph of the Kerry landscape: amazingly, the wild and wonderful scenery and the unpredictable weather are noticeably missing from his imagery. But maybe this is not really so surprising, since he describes his work as "dealing intimately with *life* in the Irish countryside."

What makes George Fitzmaurice uncommon is that he is writing of himself. He is dramatizing his experience as it had never been done before. There have been many movements, particularly in the late nineteenth century, to "go down to the people" and express their life as they themselves cannot do it. The end result is that such writers see themselves or express themselves in peasant dress, just as Fitzmaurice's peasants saw not real royalty, but themselves as royal. But George Fitzmaurice, avoiding movements, developed a local and personal form of drama, yet managed to go beyond himself and County Kerry.

CHAPTER 4

Dramatic Techniques: Conventional and Experimental

FROM the start, the Irish Literary Theatre had been conceived as an experimental theater, and not merely as an instrument of the Celtic Revival. Yeats made this aim clear in everything he wrote about the theater. "We hope to find in Ireland ... that freedom to experiment which is not found in the theatres of England, and without which no new movement in art or literature can succeed."[1] Although this statement overlooks J. T. Grein's Independent Theatre, a London experimental art theater established in 1891, the oversight is probably deliberate, for the Irish Theatre was established partly as a reaction to the so called naturalism and didacticism of Ibsen and Shaw who were the first dramatists produced at Grein's theater. Yeats experimented with various techniques throughout his playwriting career: he began by writing nationalistic plays in prose like *Cathleen ni Houlihan* and in verse like *The Countess Cathleen;* he turned out plays in blank verse about Celtic myths, using Cuchulain *(On Baile's Strand)*, and Deirdre *(Deirdre)*; he experimented with highly stylized lyric plays based on the ancient Japanese Noh tradition in plays like *Calvary* and *The Resurrection.* Lady Gregory , too, had experimented with her folk history plays, wonder plays, and translations of Molière into Kiltartan. She herself remarked, "The desire to experiment is like fire in the blood."[2]

George Fitzmaurice experimented, too. It was the stimulus of the literary revival that first attracted Fitzmaurice to the theater, but not long after he started writing plays, the stage lost interest in him. He contributed plays to *The Dublin Magazine,* where they appeared intermittently between 1924 and 1954. J. D. Riley, responding to these published plays, as well as to the four Abbey productions, wrote of Fitzmaurice: "I believe he emerges as an artist of stature, and that in recording his vision with such good-natured fidelity he has become Ireland's most adventurous and successful experimental dramatist."[3] These are strong words, especially in light of the quantity and quality of plays produced in Ireland in the first half of the twentieth century.

Fitzmaurice wrote folk plays which, when successful, dramatized the living folk imagination of Kerry in their fusion of peasant superstition with everyday farm life. Fitzmaurice's legendary figures are always conceived of in a small-town context. His dramatic techniques in staging his folk vignettes are unique in that he has tried to preserve the folktale as nearly as possible in its distinctive narrative form, and yet mold that form into drama. Moreover, Fitzmaurice presented his audiences with dark and somber plays when they were led to expect comedy— this resulting from his habit of inserting considerable harshness into a comic framework. He often dramatized symbols which focused the spectators' attention on the plays' central themes, even though the symbols themselves are often open to differing interpretations. He consistently mingled realism with fantasy. And finally, the characters of Fitzmaurice's fantasies are no longer realistically motivated but are manipulated to demonstrate the author's case. George Fitzmaurice was writing at a time when delight in folklore and folk idiom was both genuine and formative, and his experimental dramaturgy is a curious outgrowth of this activity.

I   *Realistic Plays:* The Country Dressmaker

Fitzmaurice started out in a more or less conventional way. His first Abbey production, *The Country Dressmaker*, is a realistic comedy. The play was and still is very popular, one of the most frequently revived of all the Abbey plays. On the surface it is a delightful romantic comedy concerning Julia Shea who gets her sentimental ideas of love from reading popular magazines like *The Family Reader*. But beneath the surface, the play depicts a tension between illusion and insight or between dream and reality.

Julia has been pining for Pats Connor, who emigrated to America ten years earlier. She has endowed him with all the qualities of the novelette hero and has cherished the illusion that he intends to return to Ireland to claim her for his bride. Ellie Clohesy has conspired to foster this deception, and ironically it is this very cruelty which ultimately leads to Pats' and Julia's marriage. Without Pats' bogus letters which Ellie periodically "produces" in order to fool Julia that Pats' "whole study in America was to make a pile for her," Julia probably would have married Edmund Normyle. Because of her hero worship, Julia has forestalled Edmund's attentions. When the play's course of action shows us Pats' return, it is obvious that he had not thought of Julia Shea very often. But when he learns that Julia has been waiting for him, he pretends that Ellie's hoax has been the truth. Julia is somewhat dismayed by Pats' altered appearance, but the second act ends with the young couple's marriage assured. The third act discloses several troublesome situations, two of which have been hinted at in act 2: the Clohesys' last ditch effort to win Pats away from Julia, Pats' past marriage to another woman, but most important, Julia's disenchantment with Pats. The play ends with Julia deciding to accept Pats and with him a reality less exciting than her dream.

The comedy seems conventional enough, but actually it is not typical of romantic comedy. Normally tension arises from external obstacles deliberately set up to block the final pairing. In *The Country Dressmaker* the obstacle to Julia's and Pats' marriage is internal: it is the dressmaker's disappointment that Pats has not lived up to her ideal; he has not been the devoted lover. This is why, after ignoring his attentions, she suddenly regrets losing the devotion of Edmund Normyle, who, if nothing else, has been the constant lover. And beneath all this is the disillusionment of what ten years have done to Pats' handsome looks. The main structural problem for a play like this is to successfully dramatize disillusionment.

The comedy is successful. The characters are carefully drawn. Julia, for instance, could easily have degenerated into a figure of farce or caricature, had Fitzmaurice's object been romantic comedy. Instead, Fitzmaurice converts her simplicity into insight. The delight in extravagant character, which will become more pronounced in the fantasies, is evidenced here in the matchmaker, Luke Quilter. The language is a richly poetic dialect. But *The Country Dressmaker* falters structurally because it is not clear what brings about the play's crisis (Julia's disillusionment), precisely because of Fitzmaurice's difficulty in making the abstract concrete. (Interestingly, he has no such difficulty in his best fantasies, probably because of the way he dramatizes in each a central symbol which clarifies the play's meaning.) Something has happened between acts 2 and 3 to change the course of the play's action, as Julia is no longer willing to marry Pats Connor. Her difficulties are suggested in act 2, but too inconspicuously. Joseph Holloway, in writing about the opening night of *The Country Dressmaker*, noticed this weakness: "There was an absence of curtains about the comedy; each act ended somewhat tamely I thought, and the second was not nearly so well constructed nor real to us as the first and last acts."[4] Fitzmaurice must have felt this way too, for he subsequently changed the ending of the second act. All published versions of the play which precede the 1970 Dolmen publication show the following ending to act 2:

(Exeunt Michael, Maryanne and Ellen)
BABE: It's some harm I did. I'm thinking, by what I told him. But how could I help it with the cute old withered sham of a Yank and the way he pretended to be enjoying it. *(Goes Out)*

After Fitzmaurice's death the 1921 Maunsel and Roberts edition of *The Country Dressmaker* was found in his room. It was marked up, revealing a number of changes, the most striking of which is the strengthening of the second-act ending. Fitzmaurice substituted the following for Babe's final speech:

BABE: I have done harm coddled by that old sham of a Yank. I'll do more harm or something will give. I'll break the chaney taypot. *(Handles teapot, reflects and replaces it on a little table.)* *(Suddenly)* I wo-ant; I wo-ant. *(Bursts out door slamming it after her. As curtain falls noise of broken crockery is heard.)*

Babe's "I'll do more harm" relates to her mother's last statement, "He's not gone from us till he's married to her," and her father's last line, "If we could only get him in the clutches of the Clohesys." In one way, this new ending is a better transition into act 3 than the one Holloway saw at the Abbey in 1907, for it anticipates the third act which will show another attempt by the Clohesys to get their man. But in another far more important sense, the changed ending aborts an important transition which was present in the first version. In the first version, "the old withered sham of a Yank" stresses Pats' physical deterioration, a terrible jolt to Julia's romantic dream. To delete this in the final rendition is to weaken the shift from the second to the third act.

The central thematic issue in *The Country Dressmaker* is Julia's discovery and acceptance of life as it is rather than as she wants it to be. The situation which evokes her insight is her disillusionment with Pats Connor when she meets him after a ten years' absence, a very different man from her imagined suitor. It is only at the very end of act 3 that we know positively that it was this first shock of seeing Pats after ten years that changed Julia's opinion of him: "Not because of the German woman, Min—for now I confess all to you—or crime might have done, but because he is what he is and isn't what he was, Min. Love died the first minute I saw him at Clohesys, and my dreams for ever were over." It is Pats' altered appearance which "killed" Julia's love. In the first act, Julia, in talking to Min, makes it very clear that what she loves about Pats is his handsomeness.

MIN: Some say he was a vain little fellow, then, a little dandy, as proud of his curls as a peacock. 'Twas said he used the curling tongs itself on a pattern day or going to a dance.

JULIA: Backbiters! 'Twasn't in need of the curling tongs he was, the curls fell in pure little natural waves down on his forehead, and he used always wear the cap back on his poll.

MIN: Psough! I never like to see curls on a boy.

JULIA: There are curls and curls. If I could describe to you Pat's!

In act 2, it is obvious Pats has lost his curls. Julia's initial reaction to seeing her long absent "lover" is dismay: "So changed, so changed! When Sir Geoffrey came back there was no change in him but the grey hair on his temples. Can that be Pats?" The physical change is obviously more noticeable than a few grey hairs; it seems very likely he has come back bald or at least partially bald. Julia speaks to Pats only three more times in act 2. After Pats complains that "there is no smile of welcome for me after all these years," Julia replies that it is because their reunion is so unexpected. Then she says that she is not deserving "to share your pile." Pats does not take this to be romantic reluctance on Julia's part, but her "dear Irish bashfulness." He kisses her and announces that this is the happiest day in both their lives. Julia answers, "Yes, Pats." Presumably Pats and Julia will wed and live "happily after after."

The third act opens on this note of impending wedded bliss: Luke Quilter, Matt Dillane, and Norry Shea happily plan the wedding. But as the action progresses, Julia spoils it all by regretting the loss of Edmund.

It's a terrible thing I have done. It's for this man that I scorned the heart that cherished me.... It's the bad treatment I gave Edmund after all his love and devotion to me. A Friday he came here looking at me, to see if I was happy, and he knowing the reports that were going around. A harsh look and a short word were his thanks, for the pride and bitterness were strong in my heart. I told him to hurry and marry Bridget Gildea and not to be coming here anymore, and it's to please me he's marrying her to-day.

Julia has already learned of Pats' American marriage when she speaks these lines. It is entirely in keeping with her character that she thinks of all the love and devotion Edmund gave her since she now realizes Pats was not romantically faithful. The point is, this line of motivation, if placed in act 2 rather than act 3, would make for a better play. It is true that Pats' former marriage is mentioned in act 2, but this is not made important from Julia's point of view, because the fact that Michael Clohesy brings the subject up at all is Fitzmaurice's method of illustrating, once more, just how cunning the man is. "Let no one hearabouts get a hint of it, but it's up with the break of day you must be, and away with you on the horse and car to Meenscubawn. You couldn't be too cautious in dealing with Yanks, woman. It's twenty times that man might be married for himself since, unbeknownst. Tomaus must know, and the sister would pick it out of him if you could come around her at all."

It is true that there is a hint of a change in Julia's feelings for Pats in act 2, but to make this suggestion definite depends not on the text alone, but upon the talent of an actress taking her cue from act 3's "Love died the first minute I saw him," to convey the appropriate dismay. Julia is dismayed at what age has done to Pats' appearance, and she is also dismayed that he has deceived her: "It's no hint you ever gave me you were married to a German woman, Pats Connor!" But we do not discover this until act 3.

It would be better structurally to disclose Julia's reactions at the end of act 2. The issue of disillusionment followed by acceptance is the focus of the play. The disillusionment must be *unmistakable* by the end of act 2, or there is no real reason for an

act 3. The two young people are together, and that is the point of
conventional romantic comedy. The only impediment to Pats'
and Julia's happiness at the end of act 2 is the Clohesy
determination to get Pats. If the play were over at this point,
their frustrated contrivances would be acceptable as poetic
justice. They are portrayed as conniving; that they lose the game
would disturb no one. However, an act 2 ending produces a very
different play: a somewhat untidily plotted romantic comedy
which ends as romantic comedy is supposed to end—in the
lovers' togetherness. But this is not the play that Fitzmaurice
wrote nor meant to write. He wants the bittersweet compromise
for his resolution, as it is essential to his view of things. The real
structural problem, then, is not that the play should end after act
2, but that Julia's crisis of disillusionment is not made absolutely
clear until the end of act 3, or to put it another way, the problem
is solved before it is clearly defined.

Even so, the play is deservedly popular. Though Julia Shea, the
romantic dressmaker, learns to make the best of the rather sad
thing life can be, Julia and Pats are joined in the end, after all.
From the very beginning of his dramatic career George
Fitzmaurice mingles the bitter with the sweet. Although this is
romantic comedy, it ends somewhere between happiness and
pain. It is, like all else George Fitzmaurice wrote, seriocomic.

II   *Realistic Plays:* The Moonlighter

A more serious handling of the theme of disillusionment, this
time disillusionment of fidelity to an ideal rather than of
romantic love, is taken up in *The Moonlighter*. Here Fitzmaurice
is still working within the realistic mode. *The Moonlighter* is an
even more ambitious play of peasant realism than *The Country
Dressmaker*. It is Fitzmaurice's longest (four acts) and most
intricately plotted play. The play concerns the various members
of four families, all dairy farmers, and a nationalistic group called
the moonlighters. The Guerins, the Driscolls, the Carmodys, the
Cantillons, and Captain Synan and his "boys" all interact by
reason of their varying degrees of involvement in the Kerry land
struggles of the 1880s. Peter Guerin, an ardent old Fenian turned
rentwarner, a man who served rent notices for absentee
landlords, opposes his son Eugene's moonlighting activities. He
has already banished his other sons to America for taking part in

nationalist activities. The first three acts lead to the Moonlighters going off to raid the Big House. Eugene seizes a gun and
runs off to kill his uncle, Big William Cantillon, a landgrabber.
Act 4 takes place twelve months later. Big William has been
killed, Eugene has been in the city for a year, and Tom Driscoll
has been informed on as a murderer. Just before Eugene returns,
his gun is found unfired, and when he reappears he only wants to
live quietly as a farmer. When Tom comes to the Guerin cottage
to borrow a gun in order to try to escape, Eugene shows his
cowardice by hiding. But Peter's old Fenian spirit is aroused; he
rushes out to face the rifles of the police in an attempt to aid
Tom. Both men are killed, and Eugene is left to deal with the
contempt of friends and family.

Fitzmaurice touches upon many themes in the course of the
four acts. He deals with the tragedy of generations in conflict,
with ironic compromisings of principle, with patriotism, cowardice, honor, guilt, even with insanity, violence, and death.
Everyone who has written of the play faults it for just this reason:
so many themes and characters give the spectator or reader an
overall impression of disjointedness. It is true that the interest
shifts often—from one character to another: from Big William
Cantillon, a landgrabber, to Morisheen Lucy whose land is
grabbed, from Malachi Cantillon, the gombeen man, to Maura
Driscoll and Breeda Carmody, whose love for Eugene and Tom
involve them in the tragedy, from Synan, the ill-fated captain of
the moonlighters, to Ellen, Eugene's mother and to Eileen, his
sister.

That the play is crammed with diverse themes, as well as with
strong characters, cannot be denied. Even so, the play is not
disjointed. The case for coherence of *The Moonlighter* rests on a
thematic basis as well as on a central character basis, though
many critics disagree. J. D. Riley, for example, wrote in an article
in *The Dublin Magazine*, "The play centres rather loosely about
Eugene Guerin, and shows us the bravado and superficial
rebelliousness that first raises him to the status of a Playboy, but
then, collapsing, leaves him much like Donal Davoran, poltroon
if never poet. Fitzmaurice's characterization is admirable, but
here as before this interest leads him to enlarge his "lesser"
people until they tend to overshadow the rather slight figure of
Eugene."[5]

The difficulty here arises from not understanding who the

moonlighter is. The hero (or antihero) of the play is not Eugene
Guerin; it is Tom Driscoll. When Tom is seen as hero, the various
parts fit together favorably. That Fitzmaurice meant Tom to be
the hero is unmistakable: at the end of act 4 as Tom is dying and
as the neighbors read the litanies for the dead, Tom is called the
moonlighter and "it is for him and the like of him that the flowers
smile, and always smiled, in the green soil of Ireland."

Tom and Eugene occupy center stage for the first three acts.
Immediately in act 1 both are introduced by means of their
mothers' conversation. Ellen is concerned that Eugene's moonlighting activities will impel his father to send him away as he has
done with their other sons. Peg Driscoll expresses the grim
premonitions she feels about her son, Tom. Because Eugene's
family, his mother, Ellen, his sister, Eileen, his father, Peter, and
his uncles, Malachi and Big William, are so vital, both in
characters and to the plot, it seems at first glance, that Eugene
must be the protagonist. Fitzmaurice, though, very subtly reveals
a different moonlighter than Eugene. The first act ends with
Eugene and Tom racing off to a glen for a meeting with Captain
Synan and his band of moonlighters.

Act 2 leaves no doubt as to who the real hero of the play is.
Tom tells Eugene that he became a moonlighter by chance, that
he was a friend of Jamesie Quirke's who had been a member of
Synan's group for years. One night, after "a share of porter
taken," Tom joined up too. Eugene berates Tom for this lack of
glorious purpose. And yet in the glen scene Cosdee and Lucy,
two moonlighters who watch Eugene rush away from the police,
comment on his cowardliness: "and it's the gammy moonlighter
he is that didn't pause to think where to run like the rest of us,
but to bolt in disorder the way he did like a blind mad bull!"
After it is safe to emerge from hiding, Eugene comes upon his
Uncle Malachi, his mother, and his sister, all of whom he realizes
have been spying on him. To save face he pretends to thrash his
uncle. Eileen begs him to go home with her, and the act ends
with his boastful words: "I will go home then, Eileen. Be thankful
for your skin to this child, Malachi Cantillon, and never again
come spying after a national man of Ireland!" Swagger aside, the
speech is poignantly ironical. It is Eileen's screech which alerted
the moonlighters to the arrival of the peelers and it is Eileen who
is later killed trying to save Eugene's "skin." Fitzmaurice
carefully sets up a likeable and human figure in Tom, while

simultaneously revealing Eugene's intolerance and bravura. Granted, the revealing of Tom's budding heroic qualities cannot displace Eugene as protagonist. Even so, Tom is central to the action of the play as Fitzmaurice makes clear very gradually.

In act 3, Fitzmaurice builds suspense, while making point after point in favor of Tom, as he discloses Eugene's sham. The act opens with Malachi complaining to his sister Ellen about Eugene's ingratitude and phony bravery. Ellen begs Malachi not to be too "harsh with him." The protection of Eugene from everyone, but especially from Peter and Malachi, is Ellen's chief function in the play. No one protects Tom; he must stand alone. In the courtship mechanism in the same act, attention is focused on Tom to the almost total exclusion of Eugene. Tom overhears Breeda telling Maura that she is growing tired of him. His sincere love for the fickle Breeda is made very clear. The whole wooing scene centers on Driscoll integrity. Maura Driscoll truly loves Eugene, and Tom, Breeda. That the objects of their love are deficient is one more instance of how far short of the ideal life always is. The act ends with Tom and Eugene going off with the moonlighters, both in defiance of their fathers' wishes.

In act 4, when Eugene comes home after a year's absence, Peter welcomes him perfunctorily, even though Eugene promises he is through forever with any "national" activities. Shortly after Eugene's subdued homecoming, Tom Driscoll comes in asking for a gun to protect himself against the police who are chasing him. He has been accused of murdering Big William Cantillon, Eugene's uncle, whom Eugene threatened to kill a year earlier because of his landgrabbing activities. Eugene hides because he is afraid he might show the police a sympathy for Tom which he does not feel, and which might implicate him. What could have been called Eugene's Falstaffian pragmatism earlier in the play, is now outright faintheartedness. Before Tom rushes out to face the police, he tells Peter he is no longer afraid because he has had a dream in which his Uncle Martin tells him "a man of my breed" cannot be afraid. Tom's mention of his uncle rouses Peter to action, and sadly the two men are killed. The neighbors who come to pray for the dead call them the moonlighter and the Fenian man. The last speech in the play is about Tom, the brave moonlighter, the hero on whom the play is focused.

Fitzmaurice leads us to believe the moonlighter is Eugene, but

slowly and surely reveals Tom's prominence. The real skill of
this particular technique is the way it gradually becomes obvious
that Tom is the focus thematically as well as technically. The
issue of integrity or steadfastness applies to the several strands of
story interest—the father-son conflict, the patriotic sentiment,
the courtship, and the "making of a hero."

There is a conflict between Peter and his son Eugene
throughout the whole play. Peter strongly disapproves of
Eugene's moonlighting activities. And yet Peter was once an
ardent Fenian. Eugene knows this and early in act 1 accuses his
father of being a turncoat, as Peter had become a rentless warner
in 1877. This accusation anticipates the various nationalistic
reversals which shape the play's resolution. Fitzmaurice makes it
clear that Peter was not "steadfast" to his patriotic ideal because
of a need for security; he had a family to support. Malachi
describes the disillusionment Peter felt because of his lack of
integrity:

Eugene will be grateful! He will be like Peter the time I took all the
trouble to wheedle him into taking the rentwarnership and he dragged,
and all the trouble I took to keep him in it a few years itself, he chafing
against it and ashamed; meantime I had to be telling big lies to the
agent that the reason he wouldn't attend eviction was because you
were too national in yourself, moryah! And when he flung it up in the
finish, he starts cursing me for my zeal and my ingenuity, and he rearing
again against the Cantillons.

This speech looks forward to Peter's Fenian conversion at the
end of the play. By the end of act 3, Peter is singing Fenian songs,
yet despite his incipient patriotism, he still objects to Eugene's
exit with Captain Synan and the moonlighters. Act 3 ends with
Peter announcing he will send to America for his son Luke;
Eugene is gone, and Peter does not really care, for it is Luke he
really loves.

Early in act 4 we learn why Luke is his father's favorite. Peter
quotes from Luke's letter: "'tisn't in your power to bring me back
the same as you drove me away.... There is a future before me, I
promise you, and it don't signify now whether you'd let me be a
moonlighter or no; though it's the same hatred I have against the
landlords and the English, and the same love for the old sod I'll
likely see no more." Peter says it is the same answer he would

have made himself. Again, Fitzmaurice anticipates the conclud-
ing action of the play when Peter tries to help Tom escape the
police.

Eugene's patriotic bravura, obvious from his very first speech
in act 1, is gradually shown to be nothing more than talk. Eugene
wanted to be a moonlighter for personal glory, just as Captain
Synan used his patriotic activities as a cover up for his real
motive of avenging his sister's seduction, just as Malachi
supresses his antipathy toward landgrabbers if there is a profit in
it. All these men prostitute their patriotic ideals for personal
motivations of vanity, revenge, and economic gain. They are a
poignant contrast to Tom who never pretends to live by any
patriotic ideal. He joined the moonlighters purely by accident;
he has no great desire to be a dead hero; he looks forward to a
happy life with Breeda. And yet it is Tom who is steadfast, who
does not "sell out," and who is the real moonlighting hero of the
play. Even in the courtship scene, he is the only steadfast lover;
he is loyal to Breeda, though Breeda is "a changeable and
contrary girl."

Throughout the play, from the beginning of act 1, are
anticipations of the many ironic reversals that express
Fitzmaurice's vision of life. These many anticipations are
structural strengths, showing that Fitzmaurice is very much in
control when constructing this play. And the unity suggested
here is ultimately thematic: the issue is steadfastness. Tom
exemplifies it and the others show its reverse. Thus, the play is
not diffuse and disjointed as so many reviewers claim.

Nevertheless, the play reveals some weak points that will
recur in several of Fitzmaurice's plays. One of the most
important is that there is too much offstage action between acts 3
and 4, most of it extraneous to any plot development. Six people
are killed, one goes mad, and another turns traitor. Even so, *The
Moonlighter* is, as *The Evening Mail* called it, a triumph: "It is a
play of tense situations, of real character, of emotional power
and pungent phrase, drawn from the history and life of the
country. The question that must be asked is why should the
National Theatre have rejected and suppressed this play by a
fine dramatist for all these years."[6] *The Country Dressmaker* and
The Moonlighter, a "comic" and a "tragic" example of conventional drama, establish George Fitzmaurice's credentials as a
successful playwright of realism.

III   *Transition from Realism to Fantasy:* The Pie-Dish

Another very early play, *The Pie-Dish* is a kind of transitional play, based not on the realism of *The Country Dressmaker*, nor on an all out fantasy like *The Enchanted Land*. It represents a definite move toward the folk view of things in presenting an essentially tragic theme in comic dress.

The play was a total failure with its first Dublin audience. The newspapers unanimously condemned it, probably because of a misunderstanding of the play: the audience expected comedy and yet witnessed tragic actions. Much of *The Pie-Dish* is comic in its colloquial blending of the funny and sad, but more, there are farcial dimensions which elicit a comic response. The play opens with Eugene's and Jack's attempts to put their grandfather, who is sleeping in a chair, in a settle bed (a wooden sofa kept in the kitchen which unfolds into a bed). Their mother wants him settled for the priest who is coming to give the dying Leum the last rites, but his grandsons know that if he awakens he will not cooperate with them as he will want to work on his pie-dish. So they hope to trick him by getting him in the bed before he awakens. The manner and mood in which the brothers discuss their grandfather's pie-dish while they move him to the bed is more comic than tragic. While Leum sleeps, the brothers, and their mother and aunt, who enter after Leum is put in the settle bed, discuss the man and his eccentricities. This too, while exhibiting pathetic undertones, is more comic than tragic. When Leum finally wakes up, and the play is more than half over at this point, an audience is bound to see Leum humorously. And finally, the caricature of Father Troy, though meant as a satirical thrust at the conforming and constricting influence of the church, would convince the Abbey audience the play is supposed to be a comedy.

And yet Leum Donoghue has worked for twenty years, and meditated for thirty years before that, about his pie-dish. He began his great work when he realized his daughter, Johanna, was tired of having him about, and it was then he slept out one night in the dreaded fairy fort and in the morning went to live with his daughter Margaret. It was at this time he began fashioning his pie-dish which was to represent for Leum all the meaning and beauty of his earlier and happier life. Leum tries to make his favorite grandson, Eugene, understand what his creation means, but Leum knows it is only his three living contemporaries who can understand his vision, no doubt because they too harbor regret.

As the play progresses, Margaret and Johanna try to keep Leum in bed, anxious about his making a pious end, but he defies them to work on his pie-dish. The priest arrives, and after hearing about Leum's pie-dish making, thinks him possessed by a devil. Leum, who is sinking fast, begs God for time to finish his life's work. As he grows weaker, he invokes the devil for time. He falls dead after his diabolical invocation, and the dish shatters on the floor. The priest announces Leum's damnation, while Margaret prays it will not be so. There is nothing funny about any of this, nor did Fitzmaurice mean it to be funny.

Fitzmaurice baffled his audience by presenting an essentially tragic theme within a comic framework. The semifarcial capers of putting Leum in a settlebed, his confused awakening, and the caricature of the priest invite comic response. The discovery of Leum's desperate attempt to find some meaning and understanding in a hostile world through his creation suggest serious and even tragic overtones, which are incongruous with the earlier framework.

It is the new "form" which makes *The Pie-Dish* so very different from his earlier realism. Moreover, the intense significance given to rather absurd actions, which we never fully understand, is a slant away from realism. For example, Fitzmaurice mystified his audience by his choice of a pie-dish as his central symbol. What does the symbol mean? Is Leum an artist creating his masterpiece; or is he the visionary hemmed in by an unachieved dream; or is he the escapist running from the dull routine of farm chores; or is he all three? The symbol, then, could be the art work, or the goal which sets him above his neighbors, or the drug which allows him to escape a pallid everydayness. The whole of the action surrounding the central symbol is mysterious, and at first sight unmotivated and nonsensical. The presence of the priest as a figure representing the prohibiting and restricting influence of the church suggests Leum as artist. The hostility of his environment hints at Leum as visionary, inasmuch as any nonconformist evokes hostility. The reason he finally began working on his dish after thinking about it for thirty years—because he no longer felt welcome with Johanna—presupposes Leum as escapist. That Leum never finishes his dish assumes all three interpretations: what is important is the making of the dish; it gives his otherwise unbearably lonely life meaning. He is surrounded by obtuse and unsympathetic people so what he dreams will be his masterpiece is an outlet for his sensitive soul. He dreams of capturing lost happiness, and the dream encompasses art, vision, and escape. We can only surmise this from the overall tragic feeling we have about Leum and his fate. If Leum were escapist only, the play would be pure comedy or farce. That it is not indicates an open-ended interpretation for the pie-dish symbol. The play ends with the same question with which it began: "But what was in this at all? What was in this at all?"

The Pie-Dish is a kind of halfway house between Fitzmaurice's conventional dramaturgy and his more experimental folk fantasies. Margaret's cottage, the settle bed, and the farm chores are real enough, for that matter so are Margaret and Johanna. But Leum Donaghue is not a full bodied character in the realistic tradition; we do not know what motivates him; we must surmise. He is a very early example of a type Fitzmaurice manipulates in order to show what happens to a sensitive person who is opposed by family (no one even tries to understand him), by church (Father Troy can only think Leum must be possessed by a devil), and by superstition (Leum was "always an industrious man about the fields" until the night he spent in the fairy fort).

To sum up, the tragicomic ambivalence of *The Pie-Dish* obviously baffled audiences. Equally confusing are the interpretive suggestions which define the play. Supposedly shedding light upon its meaning is a dish which seen from Leum's point of view is a talisman against disenchantment, but from Father Troy's and his family's perspective is the work of the devil. The pie-dish is deliberately suggestive, leading as it does to such allusive symbols as magic glasses and dandy dolls which elucidate more by hinting then explaining. This is fitting, for intimation rather than explanation is characteristic of the folk imagination.

IV   *Plays Exhibiting Innovative Techniques*

Fitzmaurice's experimentation consists of his attempt to express dramatically segments of this folk imagination, an experimentation Austin Clarke noted some thirty years ago. He wrote:

The need for a new Irish imaginative drama has become a recurrent topic. It must have occurred to everyone, for instance, that our folklore could have inspired a dramatist in more ways than one. Ibsen interpreted the Norwegian folk mind in his early poetic dramas and his example is still an excitement to the fancy. Synge displayed the imagination of the folk in its clash with reality, but he wrote within the limitations of a closed form. Who would take the next step forward, break through the form into a more experimental one, show now only the folk but the peopling of their imagination, make visible those fancies and meanings which are older than the pot on the hook or the poteen bottle in the hedge? One writer took that step, took it at what seemed the right time and, given full opportunity, might have given another twist to folk drama.[7]

What exactly does Mr. Clarke mean by writing Synge "wrote within the limitations of a closed form"? Does he mean that Synge used folk tales, but as the basis of traditionally constructed plays? And if so, what is a traditionally constructed play? The implication is George Fitzmaurice worked on some other form. What form? How can a dramatist, as Clarke describes Fitzmaurice, show the peopling of the folk imagination? And what "twist" does Clarke envision Fitzmaurice might have given to folk drama? It is important to answer these questions if one wants to analyze Fitzmaurice's dramatic experimentation. Clarke continues by saying that Fitzmaurice experimented with Irish folklore in a difficult, precarious art form. Precisely what Clarke means is difficult to say. It is true that instead of our being told about various fairy beliefs in the course of a Fitzmaurice play, the beliefs are actually dramatized before our eyes. In *The Dandy Dolls* the Hag of Barna swoops down on the stage. The Linnaun Shee appears at Jamesie Kennelly's kitchen door. A mermaid can be heard flopping along a road in *The Green Stone*. Twelve-toed Elaine is a real creature of the ocean. That these creatures of Irish folklore are dramatized, however, does not demonstrate a difficult or precarious art form. Wild fairy-tale figures have been staged for centuries. What Austin Clarke was getting at can best be expressed, perhaps, by another critic, J. D. Riley, who differentiates between peasant and folk drama, naming the realm of the folk play the exclusive dramatic property of George Fitzmaurice. The folk tale "contains a mite of hard and significant reality so layered over by imagination ... that its origins are almost wholy obscured." The problems of peasants are presented realistically while the folk

express them obliquely in imaginative fantasy. ... Folk drama presents
not only the experience, but also the germination and growth of the
significant tale that arises out of the experience. ... At its most
successful the folk drama achieves a remarkable synthesis of realism
and fantasy, while its failures are marked by a general obscurity and
lack of form. Fitzmaurice's aim has been to recreate the folk tale so
nearly as possible in its distinctive narrative form, but to render this
form dramatic in effect. ... The result ... has been his independent
development of an experimental method that is quite as unusual as his
aim. It is in form and technique that his work stands most noticeably
apart, and it is by his success in setting up the stage a part of the living
folk imagination that he alone has realized one of the more important
aims of any national literary movement.[8]

The dramatization of folktales recreated in their distinctive
narrative form, as well as the staging of a part of the living folk
imagination is probably what Austin Clarke meant when he
wrote that Fitzmaurice experimented with a difficult, precarious
art form. The very nature of the dramatic form is opposed to the
heavily descriptive narrative which forms a major part of most of
Fitzmaurice's folk plays. His occasional success in this curious
mode, in plays like *The Magic Glasses* and *The Dandy Dolls*, is
remarkable. The very form of the folktale is dependent upon the
fact that it belongs to an oral tradition; a long expository section
followed by a short climatic action is essential to the storyteller's
art. Not only did Fitzmaurice dramatize the "form" of the
folktale, but he staged the "living folk imagination" in the way in
which his legendary figures are envisioned: the small-town
context for the hags and mermaids, the mixing of shees with
butter churns, the witch as real as the priest, the magic stone as
solid as the hearth. This combination of the real and the fantastic
is native to the Irish folk imagination. The fantastic we
understand: fairies, fairy forts, and the like are not part of the
real world, but why did Fitzmaurice not employ total fantasy?
Yeats explained why he thought fantasy must mingle with the
real. "No conscious invention can take the place of tradition, for
he who would write a folk tale, and thereby bring new life into it,
must have the fatigue of the spade in his hands and the stupors of
the field in his heart."[9] Because the folktale belongs to the group
rather than to the individual, and because it was handed down by
word of mouth, seems almost to guarantee it will always come
trailing mystery and fantasy, but as Yeats has said, without a

thorough grounding in the Irish earth as well as in Irish mist, the tale will not represent the real peasant.

Ireland is one of the last homes of the oral traditions of prehistoric and medieval Europe. Fitzmaurice has dramatized fragments of this tradition in the way he mirrors rural life always from the point of view of the folk, and in the way he sets up the deeds of his half legendary figures, again, always from the perspective of the peasant.

If there is any generalization possible, it is that folktales are often success stories, success achieved not through merit but by luck or cunning. Perhaps this explains their appeal to hard-pressed and luckless peasants. In this respect Fitzmaurice departs from the folk-tale norm, at least in most cases, for success is an inappropriate resolution for a man writing about life's compromised ideals. His folk characters are not successful, nor are they full bodied as are the realistic characters of *The Country Dressmaker* and *The Moonlighter*.

V   *Innovative Techniques*: The Magic Glasses

The Magic Glasses is an example of Fitzmaurice's "new" dramatic techniques. The play begins in Padden Shanahan's kitchen, a real peasant's kitchen, the room where most of the living is done in rural Kerry. There is a long expository section, actually more than two-thirds of the playing time, during which Padden and Maineen discuss Morgan Quille whom they have summoned to lure their son Jaymony from his top loft where he gazes into three brown, three blue, and three red glasses, while living in a fanciful world of riches and wonder. This long exposition, essentially undramatic, is as animated as the action for which it prepares us because Fitzmaurice is able to transfer characteristics of the folktale to the exposition—exaggeration, superstition, a joy "in the telling" of anecdotes.

PADDEN: ... the way he [Quille] managed Looney Carroll, chasing him through a wood in the dead hour of the night till the fool ran up again a tree unbeknownst, was flung back on his back, the blood of a pig spouting out of his nostrils, and signs by, the fool won't go round a tree since, and it stuck in him that every tree has got a divil. A queerer thing itself he did on Josie Patt. Hit him on the head with a mallett, I hear, when the big tongue was out and the teeth coming together—the Lord save us, half the big tongue was out and the teeth coming together—the Lord save us, half the big tongue fell down on the ground!

MAINEEN: A likely story! And Josie's people blowing about Mr. Quille all over the world, nothing in their mouths but that blue lozenge, talking of it from dusk till dawn at every hour of the day.

PADDEN: Because they believed Mr. Quille, and Josie can't tell whether or which, and nothing but gibberish coming from him since. Sure, they went to Mr. Quille about the way he was pronouncing, and what did my boy say but that it was French he was talking—that they all speak French for a while after being cured—and he'd come into English again in the course of forty weeks. And, when this Mr. Quille comes along, I'm thinking it's wise people we'd be if we put the bed and dresser to the door and keep the divil out.

The combination of outrageous "remedies" with a sense of skepticism about Quille's powers, plus a superstitious belief in them at the same time, points to the kind of comic insight one finds in the folk mind. Maineen's and Padden's discussion of Quille is as memorable as his actual appearance. The anecdotes about him establish him as the Braggart Witchdoctor, a variant of the comic standby, the Great Impostor—in turn the theatrical descendant of the parasite-slave of Plautus and Terence. Quille belongs to the type represented by the Jonsonian mountebank, a type perfect for the peasants' needs. What other type of character could hope to successfully oppose the "supernatural" influence of the brown woman's magic glasses on Jaymony?

The fantastic Quille finally arrives. Padden and Maineen beg his help in enticing their son Jaymony into leaving his dream-world in the top loft for the real world of farming and marriage. Quille sets out to defeat Jaymony's supernatural magic (he got his vision-producing glasses from a brown woman) with his own magic, outdoing his patient's visions with greater wonders and tempting him to exchange his fantasies for a useful, normal life. Finally, Jaymony decides to try the real world, only to discover it is nothing but "slush—same old thing every day—this an ugly spot, and the people ignorant, grumpy and savage." At the first intrusion of cold, hard reality in the arrival of his two brothers, he retreats to the loft, much to the consternation of his parents who have told everyone about Jaymony's "cure." Their attempts to bring him back to the everyday world result in the onstage destruction of the loft and the accidental death of Jaymony.

Jaymony is killed by his magic glasses: his jugular vein is cut by the broken glass. The "action" occurs in the last two pages of the script!

Quille as Celtic witch doctor is a caricature and his fabulous exoricsm to convert Jaymony from dreaming to reality is farcical. Even the catastrophic ending, the collapse of the loft, is more akin to comedy or to farce than to tragedy. And yet, like *The Pie-Dish*, *The Magic Glasses* reveals a bitter theme embodied in seemingly inappropriate comic action. It is curious the way black superstitions and death are accommodated within a comic framework. There is nothing funny about a middle-aged bachelor's inability to face reality. Jaymony has spent most of his life in a loft gazing at magic glasses wherein he sees beautiful visions, enabling him to live a dream life far more exciting than anything the real world could offer him. Jaymony did emerge from his dreamworld at puberty, for about a year, only to return to his loft where he has stayed for more than twenty years. When he is forced to come down to eat, he gets "as peevish as a cat always when coming out of that top loft."

Jaymony, like Leum, is the nonconformist, the visionary, the escapist, the sensitive man opposed by his environment and by the supernatural. His parents cannot understand a dreamer; it is Frynk and Robin, both London peelers, whom they appreciate. The "supernatural" brown woman sold him glasses which not only prevent him from living in any real sense, but in the end cause his destruction. The glasses as a symbol are different from Leum's pie-dish; they are not a symbol for the art work, but they are a symbol for the dream. Jaymony struggles against demands to make his vision fit others' standards. Of course this is what Leum is doing also; this is a theme which runs throughout many of Fitzmaurice's plays. But on the other side of the coin is the necessity for accepting the duller realities of everyday life. Jaymony's refusal to accept life with all its compromised ideals (the difference between the dream and the reality) and with all its disappointments (his parents' preferring Jaymony's two practical brothers) on any but his own terms ends in his being killed. Perhaps Fitzmaurice, who so often writes of the sadness of compromised ideals, was saying that to accept them is the only way to survive. Jaymony is a manipulated man who expresses Fitzmaurice's view that it is well to be a dreamer, but the dreamer must accept a portion of reality, too. The 1913 London production by the Abbey Company changed the ending: instead of the glasses slashing Jaymony as the loft collapses, Jaymony simply takes his glasses and leaves the house. The changed ending, while easier to stage, alters the meaning of the play.

Fitzmaurice's experimental methods in *The Magic Glasses* succeed rather well. In presenting Jaymony's story in the essentially narrative form of the folktale, he displays his predilection for the long expository section (Maineen's and Padden's and finally Quille's conversations) followed by a short climactic action (Jaymony's departure and almost immediate return to the loft, followed by its collapse). He portrays folklore, myth, and the peasant mind in long passages of descriptive dialogue which seem to go nowhere. For example, in one long section of the dialogue between Padden and Maineen, Padden tries to hide before Quille arrives, but Maineen will not permit him to go. At first glance the long section seems silly and boringly undramatic, but on closer examination one sees that Fitzmaurice is revealing the peasant mind. We are shown the peasants' partial intellectual disdain of fraudulent quacks (Quille) and superstitions (the fact they think Jaymony is possessed), yet emotionally their fear indicates more than half-belief. And later, their total acquiesence in Quille's prescriptions for Jaymony's "cure" displays their naiveté and superstition. Quille, by means of potions and pig Latin, is able to "bowl them over." And finally, in the play's fine blending of the reality of Padden Shanahan's cottage with the fantasy of a brown woman who sells magic glasses and of devils who live in top lofts, Fitzmaurice is exhibiting a part of an ancient Irish folk tradition—the pervasive mingling of the real and the fantastic.

VI *Innovative Techniques:* The Dandy Dolls

This colloquial blending of the real and the fantastic, a synthesis, it seems, native to the Irish "folk-view," is at its consummate best in *The Dandy Dolls*. *The Dandy Dolls* is more fantastic than *The Magic Glasses*, yet it too is set in a peasant's kitchen. At the opening of the play there is a true domestic scene: Cauth is sitting at the fire, knitting. Her child is on the hob. But right from the beginning the fantastic materializes in the person of the Grey Man, "one of the three Grey Men ... who dwell in that rock in the heart of the fearsome Bay of Doon, and come out of the battlements terrifying the people when the sea is roaring in the wild and dreary nights." In spite of "something queer" about the Grey Man, he and Cauth gossip a great deal. Fitzmaurice conveys a sense of folktale narrative in Cauth's speeches by her exaggerations and her superstitions, and by her verve in describing all the various "doings" of her "mangy vomiting snooker" husband. Cauth tells the Grey Man that Roger does not support her, that she and her child are hungry, that there is a leak in the roof that needs repairing, and that when Roger is not making dolls he is on the prowl for poultry.

Most of the play consists in this type of narrative exposition, cataloging Roger's iniquities and the troubles he causes his family. But in the unfolding of this narrative, Fitzmaurice gives us a picture of legendary figures as the folk see them. The hag's son steals all of the dolls' windpipes, necessitating another try at creation on Roger's part. The Grey Man, who comes to buy Roger's newest doll (but the doll must have its windpipe intact), spends his time flirting with Roger's wife.

The "action" does not begin until very near the end of the play when both the Hag and her son swoop down and the Coonihans join the battle with Father James and everyone else, until, in a wild onstage free-for-all of shouting and blows, Roger is carried off by the Hag and her son to their den in the Barna Hills. In this farcically macabre scene, the hovel goes up in smoke. The explosion is caused by a magic bottle the Grey Man of Doon gave Roger.

The conclusion is perfect: where else could Roger continue making better and better dandy dolls than with the Hag and her son? Moreover, Roger, a noncompromiser, cannot survive in a real world. From a realistic point of view, Cauth and her child are well rid of him, and the priest's flock is safe from Roger's nightly raids. Curiously, the resolutions of *The Pie-Dish* and *The Magic Glasses* remove us from the folktale world, but with *The Dandy Dolls,* the play ends in a fantasy world.

Without its farcical elements, things like onstage battles, caricatures, comic dialogue, the play would be a tragedy, or at least a melodrama of the way humans seek an unachievable perfection. Roger Carmody is obsessed by his passion to create, yet is opposed by both supernatural and human beings. He is thwarted by domestic forces (Cauth and his child), by the church

(Father James) and by the superstitions and fairy lore of his native culture (the Hag and her son). The semilegendary forces of the Hag of Barna and the three Grey Men of Doon fight for Roger's dolls. The priest tries to rout the forces of superstition by baptizing Roger's latest doll, but his exorcism fails. Roger has sacrificed his family to his doll making, and yet not one doll has he ever sold: "He can't renayge himself to put a sop in the thatch, fix a hoop in that leaking oven, or settle a pothooks on which to hang the pot. He don't earn as much as a shilling in the week."

None of this is comic, yet the overall effect of the play is whimsy. And no wonder: the hero, Roger, steals poultry when he is not making dolls. He hides under the bed everytime the "Barna brat" comes for a newly creat ed doll. The climax of the play, the battle for the newest doll, is pure farce. Roger's wife, Cauth, the priest, Keerby, Timmeen, and the Hag's son chase each other around a table, all pulling on the doll and hitting each other. The Hag's arrival adds to the confusion.

Roger, like Leum and like Jaymony, is different from those around him, so he is misunderstood. And like Leum and Jaymony, he ignores the pressing demands of everyday life to devote himself single-mindedly to his ideal, the making of a perfect dandy doll. Roger is a character type more than a fully motivated figure such as Julia Shea of *The Country Dressmaker* or Peter Guerin of *The Moonlighter*, for here again Fitzmaurice is more interested in depicting the folk imagination within an essentially narrative folktale form, than he is in portraying a fully realistic scene, so Roger is manipulated to make Fitzmaurice's appropriate points. But Roger is more of a clown than Leum or Jaymony, both of whom are rather pathetic. No doubt he had to play the buffoon in order to compete with the wild and contorted characters that show up in *The Dandy Dolls*. Because these antiheroes, like Leum Donoghue, Jaymony Shanahan, and Roger Carmody are not "full-bodied," not fully motivated, we view their misfortunes with a cold, critical eye; they are funny and stupid, and they act in mad ways. They are totally different from Julia Shea and Billeen Twomey and Pete Munnix and Dermot Rue Mullarkey, all characters from Fitzmaurice's realistic plays, who stoically accept less than the ideal by putting up with second best. But Fitzmaurice's "folk heroes" will not compromise their ideal: Leum will create the perfect pie-dish; Jaymony prefers the dreamworld of his loft to the "slush" of everyday life, and Roger will create a perfect dandy doll no matter if his family dies of starvation or the Grey Man or Hag kill him in his attempt or the priest prevents his capturing poultry for food.

Could it be that Fitzmaurice's own lack of acceptance is echoed throughout these three folk fantasies? Father Troy joins forces with Leum's family to induce Leum to turn away from pie-dish making to thoughts of God; Morgan Quille joins the Shanahan family to try to induce Jaymony to desert his vision; Roger Carmody is opposed not only by his family in liaison with his priest but by the supernatural forces of the Hag and her son. The intention is always to badger the visionary into conformity and to stifle his independent vision. Unlike Yeats, who ennobled his alienated characters, Fitzmaurice deflates his—which is, in a sense, surprising, since Leum, Jaymony, and Roger are somewhat like Fitzmaurice himself. Rejected by Yeats and Lady Gregory, and even by the Dublin playgoing public, he tenaciously wrote play after play throughout his long life, even though none was Produced at the Abbey after 1923. When some recognition did come to him, toward the end of his life, he held onto his reclusive ways by not attending what few plays were produced.

VII   The Linnaun Shee

The Linnaun Shee is structurally weaker than the preceding three folk fantasies precisely because Fitzmaurice's "exerimental method" does not succeed. The opening exposition, though essentially and characteristically long and narrative, portrays none of the folk imagination which keeps Fitzmaurice's previous long expositions alive. The beginning section incorporates a sketch of two butter women "chatting and confabbing," followed by the women themselves questioning why their friend, Hanora, seems so distracted. The play is about half over when we finally learn that what is bothering Hanora is that it is May Eve and the Linnaun Shee is coming to take her Jamesie.

Simple bewitchment and unbewitchment is a convention of the folktale. Obviously what Fitzmaurice means to do in this play is to dramatize this particular convention: the play is about Jamesie Kennelly, who is bewtiched by the Linnaun Shee, and who is mysteriously freed from the enchantment. But the opening exposition is so long that the Jamesie-Shee matter constitutes less than a third of the play. There is nothing uncharacteristic about this except that the first two-thirds of the play do not prepare us for the "main action." In *The Dandy Dolls* and in *The Magic Glasses* the exposition preparatory to the forthcoming action is roughly the same length as here, but in the two preceding plays the exposition is a direct and lively anticipation of what is to come. The exposition of *The Linnaun Shee* has very little to do with Jamesie and the Shee: it is actually beside the point of the play. *The Linnaun Shee* is a short one-act play, therefore in no way can the largely irrelevant and sometimes uninteresting opening section be excused on the grounds that it provides tone and atmosphere.

Late in the play we learn that "Jamesie Kennelly of all men in the world—the respectable man with the respectable wife and childe" has recently begun to brood over and consort once more with the Linnaun Shee. Suddenly Jamesie appears, and just as suddenly, the Shee. The provoking fairy mistress whom Jamesie Kennelly sees as so beautiful that he exclaims "wouldn't the sea divide in compliment ot her marvel," is revealed to be a toothless hag to the other characters. Jamesie is given an ointment for protection against the Shee, but he does not want it.

She bids him come away with her; he follows. Jamesie's brother-in-law goes to a window and describes what he can see of Jamesie and the Shee. "Gone they are and disappeared as if by magic; the strange light vanished likewise. It isn't the little high green field itself I can now see with the sudden darkening—you couldn't see your hand—all is becoming as black as jet, as black as ink. Whatever in the name of God it can mean, if it isn't the devil himself is up and about and working." When Jamesie returns to his cottage he is freed from the Shee's enchantment; he intends to return to his farm chores with renewed vigor. We do not know what has happened to Jamesie, and there is no way an audience could imagine what the offstage climax was. Jamesie Kennelly has survived some experience, but what experience? That the offstage climax is described by an observer is in itself technically unadventurous when compared to *The Dandy Dolls* where the climax, fantastic as it is, is staged for us. But *The Linnaun Shee's* chief structural weakness is that what finally happens is totally unintelligible. Even if we could *see* Jamesie and the hag obscured by a black mist, we still would not understand what it was that has set Jamesie free from the Shee's spell.

Why is Jamesie involved with the Shee? Obviously he is not

the artist, nor is he the visionary, nor is he an escaptist; he is not
like Leum of Jaymony or Roger. Thematically, *The Linnaun Shee*
deals with the lost joys of youth. Jamesie had been bewitched by
the Shee before he was married. Now he is fifty-five, but he
deplores rapidly advancing age. What Fitzmaurice is trying to
convey is the sorrow every man feels for his lost youth. Sometime
in middle age each man must accept this fact of life in order to
live without lamenting over what is past. Jamesie's acceptance of
this hard truth is brought about somehow during his "cavortings"
with the Shee. But how or why we will never know. The play
fails because it is essentially a long narration; there is no real
action.

The characterization is disappointing also. The figures
portrayed are neither stock comic types nor meant as symbolic
embodiments of Fitzmaurice's vision. They are insipid and flat.
What do we know worth remembering about Bids or Den or
Daniel, or even about Hanora and Jamesie? *The Linnaun Shee* is
a disappointment after plays like *The Pie-Dish, The Magic
Glasses,* and *The Dandy Dolls.*

VIII   *A Move Toward Realism:* The Enchanted Land

The Enchanted Land is George Fitzmaurice's last attempt to
express elements of his native folklore. What makes the play an
interesting specimen is that its dramatic techniques mark a
departure from his other folk fantasies. It is only by contrasting
folk plays like *The Magic Glasses* and *The Dandy Dolls* with *The
Enchanted Land* that one can finally understand what Austin
Clarke meant when he said:

Synge had displayed in his tragedies and comedies the folk in their
clash with reality, but he wrote within the limitations of a closed form.
Fitzmaurice had been obviously excited by the example of Synge, but
was no mere imitator. He took another step forward, endeavored to
break through that form into a more experimental one, show not only
traditional life, but the figures of its legendary imaginings, making
visible those fancies and meanings which are older than the pot on the
hook or the poteen bottle in the hedge.[10]

In *The Enchanted Land* Fitzmaurice has moved away from his
characteristic fusion of long descriptive narration with short

climactic action. For this reason, the play is more conventional
then *The Magic Glasses* or *The Dandy Dolls*. (Significantly,
Fitzmaurice moves from *The Enchanted Land* back to realism in
plays like *One Evening Gleam* and *The Coming of Ewn Andzale*.)
In *The Enchanted Land* the peasant setting changes, the
dramatic action begins immediately with no preparatory exposition, and we encounter technical and thematic reversals not met
with before in a Fitzmaurice play.

To begin with, there is a variation in the usual Fitzmaurice
setting in *The Enchanted Land*: the play opens in a pure fantasy
world, and not in the customary peasant's kitchen. The first act
takes place in an underwater chamber inhabited by Grey Marse
of the Whirlpool and her husband Diarmuid. Moreover, the long
narrative exposition characteristic of Fitzmaurice is gone; the
dramatic action begins immediately and never lets up for the
three intricately plotted acts. The very first speech of the play
sets the situation.

Eithne, in proper fairy-tale fashion, has completed her
enforced stay in the underworld, exiled there for daring to love
Aeneas, the king of Ireland's son. Aeneas has now become king,
so he comes to take Eithne to the real world, Ireland, as his bride.
But Elaine, the daughter of Grey Marse of the Whirlpool and of
Diarmuid, wants to be queen of Ireland. Eithne tells Elaine to
"be contented in your own world under the sea," but the
irrepressible Elaine is not like Fitzmaurice character who
accepts second best; she outsmarts timid Eithne, steals her magic
ball of yarn which has the power to transform Elaine into a
beautiful earth woman, and takes Eithne's place in Ireland while
leaving her behind to marry Phelim of the Lobster Claws. "Win
who will and damn the misser" is the law of Elaine's life.

Act 2 takes place eight years later in the "real" world of King
Aeneas' palace. Elaine has deliberately surrounded herself by
hideous hags in order to offset her fading beauty (her stolen ball
of yarn has little magic left).

Act 3 also takes place in the palace. Kings come from all over
the world to see Elaine's famed beauty. Unfortunately for her,
the magic yarn has run out, and her beauty has vanished. Aeneas
spurns her and turns again to Eithne who has by now escaped
from the underworld. But Eithne rejects Aeneas and declares
" 'tis some satisfaction for me to know (looking at Elaine) that life
doesn't be always serene with those who follow the rule of 'win
who will and damn the misser!' " But Elaine, the villainess, is not

the "misser" after all, having put aside a bit of money for just such an eventuality. Elaine has lost her beauty, but not her ingenuity; and the play ends on this pragmatic note.

Though the first act takes place in a pure fantasy world of Grey Marse of the Whirlpool and of Maeve the Big Eel Poul-na-thoumpil in the "labyrinths of the domains of Mananaan," and though the last two acts take place in the "real" world, Ireland, the fantastic first act is written realistically while the realistic last two acts are written farcically. For example, the characters in act 1 are fully motivated; they are real in the sense that Norry Shea and Eugene Guerin are real. Eithne must wait five years for her prince charming, and while looking forward to her rescue, she entertains herself and Elaine with stories of the glory of Ireland. Elaine can never more be content in her underwater habitation, so she plots to supplant Eithne in Aeneas' affection. She succeeds by magic and by flattery: the courtiers and Aeneas are completely taken in by her deceitful adulation. In spite of the weird creatures who inhabit the domains of Mananaan, coupled with folkloric elements like the brown woman who gave Eithne her magic ball of yarn "on a haunted May Eve," the plot is not relegated to the background as in the plays like *The Dandy Dolls*. The characters and events of act 1 are well documented, and we follow the story line easily. The characters are motivated and the events are rooted in each other to form a chain of cause and effect. It is not possible to use these realistic terms in describing *The Pie-Dish*, *The Magic Glasses* nor *The Dandy Dolls*. In spite of the fantastic characters in this act, their actions are "true to life." It is in this sense that the act, though grounded in fantasy, is realistic. Fitzmaurice's practice here is parallel to the ways other Irish as well as non-Irish dramatists stage "fairy-folk" or legendary scenes.

Acts 2 and 3 of *The Enchanted Land*, situated in the palace of Aeneas, a real world in contrast to the underworld of act 1, are pure farce. The two acts evoke laughter by such devices of low comedy as the grotesque dance of the Hags, the exaggerated gluttony of Mars and Diarmuid, the magnified puerility of Aeneas, and the bombastic foolishness of the courtiers. And much of the diaglogue is right out of the music-hall tradition.

The apparent reversals in writing a scene of fantasy realistically and realistic scenes farcically mirror Fitzmaurice's story line: the usual fairy-tale theme of the beautiful and kind heroine (Eithne) rewarded for all her adversity (five years of underworld imprisonment) with marriage to the prince is turned around. The twelve-toed Elaine outwits her rival and wins the prince (King Aeneas). There is still another twist, for Elaine loses Aeneas in the end, and Eithne, finally rescued from the underworld, no longer wants him. But of course, pragmatic Elaine saves herself in the end and is well rid of the big fool, Aeneas. There are innumerable folktales in which the fool is outwitted by superior cunning—in this case Elaine's cleverness is pitted against the power of a king, and true to folkloric tradition, cleverness wins "hands down."

Fitzmaurice gives expression to the folk mind in still another way: *The Enchanted Land* sets forth royalty as the folk would imagine it—not as it really is. For one thing, all that is regal and rich in life is seen in terms of food. Marse's and Diarmuid's gluttony is immediately evident, but more subtly, Elaine imagines what life in Ireland will be like in terms of food. She dreams of "mutton and beef and venison and new milk and mead, fresh butter and honey and eggs and cheese, cakes and danties, and the divvle knows what till you had me wondering how I ever thought them fine—the boiled periwinkles they have all the mass on here or the preserved shrimps, and from the dint of listening to you even the salmon couldn't entice me in the heel, and I teetotally turned against fish." At the end of the play, when she decides to try her luck in England, she consoles herself with the expectation of enjoying better food there than in Ireland.

Another way Fitzmaurice expresses the folk mind is through his portrayal of Aeneas. Aeneas is an addlepated imbecile. His cowardice and feeble-minded opportunism make him fair game for the cunning of Elaine, and even simple-minded Eithne finally "gained a little sense," and dismissed Aeneas' "sentimental twaddle." At the very end of act 3, Elaine makes a last plea for the throne:

They are discussing Peg! Aeneas don't listen to the interested charlatans. Pull yourself together for once and be a man. . . . Get rid of these advisers and we'll reign together the two of us, and I'll exert on your behalf these wits which God gave me will make you the most powerful king on the known earth in a manner you can brandish your fist in the puss of that cowboy the King of the World himself. . . . This Peg is but a dairymaid, anyway. I may not be the wonder you thought me, but don't judge me as you would a chorus girl: I have a face good enough for a queen.

Peg, who will be the new queen of Ireland, is a dairymaid, and the point is that everyone else in the play is very much like peasant of the dairy farming class, and none more so than the king himself.

On the whole, the story line of *The Enchanted Land* with its reversals is a manifestation of Fitzmaurice's ironic imagination. There is nothing romantic or sentimental about Elaine, Diarmuid, Marse, Donal, or even Eithne. And significantly, in the end the tough-minded pragmatists triumph over all. Elaine survives because she is willing to accept second best: if she cannot hold onto the king of Ireland she will "land" an earl in England—"for an Earl over there is as big as a king here; then the roast beef is twice as good and they say there is no beating their fine cheeses."

The Enchanted Land is an apt way for Fitzmaurice to bring to a conclusion his attempt to dramatize the folk imagination: unlike Leum Donoghue, Jaymony Shanahan, and Roger Carmody, who will not compromise their ideals, Elaine, like Julia Shea and Peter Guerin, accepts what life brings and adapts herself accordingly. Over and over again we get the same idea in his plays—life is not what we want it to be, but we must make the best of it. Those who do not adapt are destroyed or spirited away to another world where presumably things will be different. There is never anything of the "and they lived happily ever after" mood about a Fitzmaurice play. Fitzmaurice portrays peasants' dreams in opposition to the reality of their lives and what happens when the two conflict. Reality always silences the dream in one way or another.

IX *Summary*

George Fitzmaurice began and ended his career writing realistic plays. His two early plays, *The Country Dressmaker* and *The Moonlighter* are far more successful than his last two, *One Evening Gleam* and *The Coming of Ewn Andzale.* In between he wrote odd little dramas which mingled realism and fantasy in a way which expressed the Irish folk tradition. His best plays are good in an unfamiliar way. What was new about them?

In his folk fantasies the sense of plot is in the background, for the inner action of the folk imagination is made vocal and narrative. The novelty consists of the way Fitzmaurice makes both the inner and outer action genuinely dramatic. The talk, which prepares the audience for the action, paraphrases fantasy, and just as in the folktale, is alive and dramatic of itself. The long exposition and the short climactic action constitute a unified whole. This is why *The Linnaun Shee* fails: the essentially narrative tale and the Jamesie-Shee action are not integrally related.

Fitzmaurice's folk characters are very theatrical (Luke Quilter, Morgan Quille, Father James); in some cases they are mannikins (Leum, Jaymony, Roger) as they represent his abiding idea that the dreamer is a rebel who must stand alone. Fitzmaurice is not psychologically realistic in his folk fantasies: he is not interested in building up spiritual biographies of his protagonists as he does in his realistic plays with characters like Tom Driscoll and Pats Connor. He is not even interested in plausibility of behavior. His chief characters are embodiments of his main ideas. The minor characters, the peasants and clergy-men, are pure victims of the Irish rural environment, and are therefore mechanized people. They too, like the dreamers, are the butt of comedy. The dreamers like Leum, Jaymony, and Roger and the mechanized people, like Father Troy, Padden, and Keerby set up Fitzmaurice's antithesis between the ideal and the real.

Farce, fantasy, realism, comedy, and tragedy, all intermingled, best convey Fitzmaurice's stoic acceptance of a very flawed humanity. In his characters' search for beauty and stability in the midst of poverty and defeat, Fitzmaurice is depicting his own vision—a vision which oscillated between fantasy and realism. The inherent ambivalence between realism and fantasy in the folk tale itself gives Fitzmaurice an appropriate medium for expressing his insight. Using the "folk imagination," he constructed his own artificial world to compensate for the real one, but he used his creative imagination less to attack and mock at the ugliness he perceived than to forge a comical world which would cancel it out.

CHAPTER 5

The Lesser Plays

N O one knows the exact chronological order of Fitzmaurice's seventeen plays. He kept no diary and left no literary pronouncements. The only surviving written material, besides his plays and stories, are a few letters, and these give no hint as to the dates of composition. However, it is possible to approximate the order in which he wrote his plays by using the dates of the four plays which were produced in the first two decades of the Abbey Theatre, the dates of the eight plays printed in *The Dublin Magazine,* and then speculate about the position of the remaining five. The following order is supposition based on these known and unknown dates.

I   The Toothache

The Toothache, not published until 1967 (in the Canadian journal, *The Malahat Review),* is probably Fitzmaurice's first play. It is a one-act farce. Patsey Dunn comes from Meenscubawn "that wild place away in the mountains" to Duagh looking for Mulcair, the smith, to pull his aching teeth. He has already visited an apothecary in Lyre for the extractions, but refused to accept treatment on the basis of the apothecary's high one shilling charge. Instead he lets the strong man of the village of Duagh pull three teeth while his cronies look on. Before, during, and after the operation, the men convince Patsey to spend nearly three shillings on porter, pushing the price of Mulcair's dental work way beyond the apothecary's.

In this play Fitzmaurice dropped phonetic spelling in his attempt to represent the Kerry dialect. The net effect of this elimination is that peculiarities of syntax are spotlighted, and it is this emphasis which makes his dialogue sound so authentic. *The Toothache* is short and slight, but bristles with fine dialogue.

PATSEY: Good morning kindly, gentlemen. Patsey Dunn is my name, and it's from Meenscubawn I come.

JIM: Why, is it now? From that wild place away in the mountains entirely?

PATSEY: It is so then, and it is every step of the twelve miles I did in less than two hours and a quarter by the sun.

JIM: And, it is to view life you skelped down here to this capital village? ...

PATSEY: It is not then, sir, though it's a grand place entirely, for 'tis hardly able I am to open my eyes atself with a head as big as a pot on me from a better of a toothache in these three teeth and you could hear the pain that's in them and they having every lep inside my head.

II   The Ointment Blue

The Ointment Blue, first performed in 1967, is an exuberant three-act comedy. Dermot Rue Mullarkey has been the champion wrestler of the "Kingdon of Carraweira" for seven years thanks to a magic blue ointment given him by the Hag of Foildarrig. Just when he needs it most he must face his toughest-opponent in Cormac O'Rourke—he has run out of the ointment. Worse, the Hag favors him no more "because he didn't mind the box he got of it but leaving the cover off and flies and every devil coming at it." As a result of Dermot's negligence, he loses the contest and the right to marry Princess Maureen.

The play is a wonderful spoof of pretension. Rich Americans are ridiculed every time references are made to the king's uncle from Texas whose sporting instincts inspired the championship contest and whose money is providing the princesses' dowries. Affectation of the upper classes is burlesqued in the king's language. Although he is named after the great king of the Red Branch saga, Conchubar, he lacks kingly attributes. He calls his queen "missus," and when he is not drinking with Priest Moore, he tries to keep her from throwing tantrums. Her guest at the contest, the Protestant bishop, is timid and silly. Unlike Father Moore and King Conacher (Fitzmaurice in this one instance reverts to phonetic spelling) who drink Irish whiskey and stay relatively sober, he drinks wine and gets very drunk. In deference to the priest, the bishop continuously chants, "Hic–Latin–haec–hoc–hic." Teig, one of Dermot's uncles, inspired by the bishop, gets carried away by his own legal jargon. Although things go badly for its protagonist, the play is a lighthearted depiction of peasants aping the gentry.

III 'Twixt the Giltinans and the Carmodys

'Twixt the Giltinans and the Carmodys, yet another instance of the matchmaking tangles of a returned Yank, premiered at the Abbey Theatre March 8, 1923, and ran for ten performances, principally because the popular actors Arthur Shields and F. J. McCormick played the one-act farce so convincingly. Lennox Robinson, the director, appears to be the only person who liked the play. The critic for *The Irish Independent* called it a "rough-house comedy," alluding to the onstage free-for-all between the Carmodys and the Giltinans who had been struggling for the past fifteen years to capture the rich bachelor Billeen Twoomey for their daughters. Billeen's unwillingness to make a final choice between Bridie Giltinan and Madge Carmody prompts an onstage confrontation. The matchmaker saves the day by chasing the competing families off the stage with a pitchfork.

In his *The Irish Drama*, Andrew Malone asserted that the comedy did nothing to enhance George Fitzmaurice's reputation. J. D. Riley, in an article on the playwright which appeared in *The Dublin Magazine*, calls the play ghoulish, basing this conclusion on the play's opening which reveals Billeen's Aunt Shuwawn sewing her shroud when the curtain rises. Maurice Kennedy in another article on Fitzmaurice in *Irish Writing* designated the play's slapdash characterization an artistic failure. Joseph Holloway in his diary entry of March 8, 1923, records, "I had tea ... before going on to the Abbey for ... George Fitzmaurice's new one-act comedy *'Twixt the Giltinans and the Carmodys*. The company played it with great farcical spirit, but could make nothing out of it, but poor talking stuff studded with outlandish words and echoing *The Country Dressmaker* at every turn."[1]

No critic commented on the play's real difficulty, namely, Fitzmaurice's use of an awkward and unconvincing device to motivate the action. Michael Clancy, the matchmaker, threatens to bring the vengeance of Thomas Brack down upon Billeen if he is not married by 5:00 p.m. Seconds before the zero hour, forty-year-old Billeen, who has deftly avoided marriage for two decades, marries the only female present, sour, dour Jane, a servant, in order to elude Brack. But who is Brack? What could he do to Billeen? That the reader or spectator does not know is a weakness in the play's structure. Thomas Brack, whoever or whatever he is functions as a flimsy deus ex machina that is not even remotely joined to the drama itself.

Andrew Malone may have been right when he mused about the possibility that Fitzmaurice wrote this play in disgust at the treatment given his fantasies. Maybe this was the playwright's attempt to give Dublin audiences and critics what they seemed to want, but if so, it was only a halfhearted endeavor because, like all other Fitzmaurice plays, it ends grimly with the newly married couple showing signs of antagonism.

IV   The Green Stone

Fitzmaurice published *The Green Stone* in *The Dublin Magazine* two years after he gave *'Twixt the Giltinans and the Carmodys* to the Abbey. In this play he presents yet another middle-aged dreamer who possess a talisman. Martineen Collopy, like Jaymony Shanahan in *The Magic Glasses*, Roger Carmody in *The Dandy Dolls*, and Jamesie Kennelley in *The Linnaun Shee* is looked upon as part visionary (his magic stone allows him to see the future), and part madman, a farmer who impertinently comments on the stupidity of the "National taychers," who flippantly calls doctors "the biggest rogues in the world," and haughtily declares that "attorneys are born damned." Afraid to destroy the magic stone because it was a gift from a mermaid, Martineen's family hides it so he will do his farm chores. When a rich American arrives to buy the stone, the family cannot find it. Unwilling to lose the sale, they substitute another stone. Martineen, disgusted by his family's obtuseness and greed, destroys the stone which disappears in an explosion of gold that is showered on the family. Everyone except Martineen and his sister, Moll Anne, will hoard the gold, indicitating their lives will be as limited and monotonous as they were before they possessed wealth.

Although all the usual devices Fitzmaurice used so successfully in his best fantasies talisman, a supernatural figure, incantatory speeches and magic tricks are present in this play, it does not measure up to the best. The dialogue, as usual, is natural, this time including language filled with American idioms like "I reckon," "I guess," "right quick," "in a jiffy."

V The Waves of the Sea

Austin Clarke maintains Fitzmaurice wrote *The Waves of the Sea* soon after he returned from France after serving with a brigade of Irish volunteers in the British army during World War I. The play is realistic except that the action is resolved by the use of a talismanic device. The first act reveals two factions of the same family fighting over land which has been willed to Rich Danagher. Rich's uncle, Wise James Danagher, cheats his nephew out of his inheritance and sends him captive to Dhoul-na-Ferris on the Isle of Doon, inhabited by the "terrible" Donal Bluebeard. Act 2 opens thirty years later, dramatizing what the ill-gotten wealth has done to the members of the Wise James' family. His sister has "the face of a spectre" because her family has become "morose and cross and queer." A niece owns a public house which causes her estrangement from her children who disprove of her selling liquor. A nephew who has become a lawyer is addicted to brandy and cannot eat. Another nephew is a glutton, "an almighty pig," and is unable to enjoy his status as a wealthy merchant. A third nephew, a country doctor, is a hypochondriac who lives in perpetual fear of dying. Near the end of the act, the tide overflows, burying the land under sand, and forcing the villagers to flee to the hills. The Isle of Doon floats to the land bringing Rich and Donal Bluebeard, now good friends, back to Kerry. In contrast to Wise James' family, they are content with their lot in life. If the play were plotted exactly as sketched here, it would be a first-rate realistic comedy, but Fitzmaurice used a magic ring to cause the flooding. The talismanic device is simply stuck on extradramatically and its use spoils an otherwise well-plotted play. As usual, the dialogue is sprinkled with the Kerry colloquialisms Fitzmaurice is so adept at reproducing: "it's a bit squeamish you are still"; "but it is a magic ring which is responsible for the flooding"; "I soon got shut of that notion."

VI The Simple Hanrahans

The Simple Hanrahans presents a variant of the marriage trick, this time without a matchmaker, in three acts. A wedding is arranged between the Hanrahan's daughter, Lena pictured by her family as virtuous, beautiful, and intellectual, able to speak French, English, and Irish, and Pete Munnix, a bachelor of thirty, so naive his mother says, "that innocent indeed that he didn't know a man from a woman." After the ceremony, Pete's family eavesdrops on the couple. From their offstage bedroom Pete relates the gradual dismemberment of his bride as she removes her wooden leg, her false teeth, and her wig. Mrs. Munnix bemoans her son's fate now that he is married to a woman in bits and pieces; her husband orders Pete to "put her together again" and return her to those "skaymers," the simple Hanrahans. Pete, dazzled by Lena's wit and charm, admits to feeling "darts of cupidity." The father must console himself with the dowry. The play is a delightful farce, marred however, by two minor characters, Billy Roche, a process server, and Jaymary Gunn, a National Teacher, who monopolize valuable playing time in endless braggadocio, a means for Fitzmaurice to satirize two types he obviously disliked. The playwright's spoofing fails as Roche and Gunn get in the way of the main plot.

VII   The Terrible Baisht

Fitzmaurice probably wrote this play long before its 1954 publication in *The Dublin Magazine*, but since it pokes fun at the pomposity of bureaucrats in the central government, he certainly was not interested in any publicity for the play before his retirement. Critics who have written about *The Terrible Baisht* fault it for having too many characters and subplots and too much stage business for a one-act play. No so; the play is an authentic picture of life in a small Kerry town and the people and plot are necessary to carry out Fitzmaurice's real purpose, which is to show the well-defined class structure and provincialism of such a town. Shannessy, the local butcher, wants to be elected representative in the Dail. He, along with the town's other leading merchants, call themselves "The Bunch." Daly, who "thinks like a poet," convinces his cohorts that the stranger in town "with an ould carbunckle on his nose" is in league with the devil. Accordingly, everyone treats the "baisht" badly. Daly decides later that the "terrible baisht" is really a clerical student and worse, the nephew of the local cannon. "The Bunch" does an about face, giving the "baisht" all sorts of merchandise including money and a leg of lamb to make up for former mistreatment and to deflect any anger the canon might feel. Actually the stranger is a tinker [a wandering gypsy] who takes advantage of his changing fortune. When "The Bunch" discovers the truth, the tinker has galloped off with his newly acquired wealth, and Daly is left to face the ridicule of his fellow merchants who blame themselves for trusting a man who has resided in Kerry only forty years.

Besides the merchants and the tinker, the characters include the town doctor, two countrywomen who comment on the action while drinking their whiskey and enjoying their "pinch" of snuff, and two farmers who discuss the incomprehensible jargon of the latest leaflet from the Department of Agriculture. This play is the only time in his career that Fitzmaurice writes about Kerry townspeople; fourteen out of fifteen plays set in Kerry depict farmers. Essentially the groups are no different, Fitzmaurice is saying; farmers and townspeople exhibit the same superstitions, ignorance, and suspicions. *The Terrible Baisht* is a delightful short piece which ought to be staged.

VIII   There Are Tragedies and Tragedies

There Are Tragedies and Tragedies is Fitzmaurice's shortest drama. The playing time for its rather static one act is fifteen minutes. Humphrey Doolen and his wife Kytie have supposedly lost 5000 pounds in a bank failure. Humphrey's brother and sister-in-law, Geoffrey and Maura, trek to Humphrey's cottage to commiserate. Geoffrey, the father of a large brood, expects to inherit his brother's land someday, a fact that is foremost in his mind when, to his disappointment, he finds his brother alive and well in spite of his recent loss. In the end, the bank failure is revealed to have been a hoax, so Humphrey's 5000 pounds is intact.

Where is the tragedy of the title? When the Doolens erroneously think they have lost their fortune, they are not especially "dazed" by their loss, but they are as concerned as ever by trivial worries—Kytie by her corns and Humphrey by his lack of suitable buttons for a new coat. What is tragic is their lack of vision and common sense; Humphrey and Kytie maintain their sterile lives with or without the money. Moreover, they are unable to recognize their shortcomings, so in a sense the title indicates a travesty of tragic heroes.

IX   One Evening Gleam

One Evening Gleam is a very strange, short, one-act play. Two old women nostalgically review the good old times they had in Dublin in younger days. As Nancy and Agnes relive the past, Agnes' forty-year-old, blind son lies nearby, dying. A neighbor, Phoebe, an alien from Sligo, interrupts their conversation briefly. Suddenly the son sees a gleam of light from a lamp, thinks he views the moon, then dies. The play ends with Agnes sitting alone with her dead son, the meaning of the play totally mysterious.

One Evening Gleam marks the first time Fitzmaurice moved a play out of Kerry, although he is writing about that part of Dublin he knew best—the respectable, lower-class neighborhoods, the music halls, and the pubs. It is curious that a man who lived more than two-thirds of is life in Dublin, located fifteen out of seventeen plays in the place of his birth.

X   The Coming of Ewn Andzale

The Coming of Ewn Andzale is Fitzmaurice's last play and the only one that ends happily. Once again the scene is Dublin, but this time the middle-class neighborhood of Rathmines. Like Fitzmaurice himself, the Davenport family are former gentry and are not happy about their present circumstances. Mrs. Davenport reviews the situation of the family beginning with "the downfall of a good old Anglo-Irish family, our beautiful country residence burnt down by the Sinn Feiners and now reduced to pinching and scraping in this little suburban house in Monkstown driven even to the deplorable extreme of having to take in those bed and breakfast people."

The family consists of Mrs. Davenport, her husband, "Captain" James, two daughters, Queenie, almost thirty and Cissie twenty-six, and a son, Popham. When the play opens Mrs. Davenport worries about how she will get her daughters married with no dowry and how Popham will earn a living, having just been fired. To give everyone hope, she writes a letter to herself from a rich, but nonexistent brother, "Ewn Andzale," in which he promises dowries for Queenie and Cissie, and capital for Popham. Just as Queenie discovers her mother's forgery, a half-brother does materialize, and he is rich and generous.

The play, Fitamaurice's worst, is mildly interesting for its autobiographical touches. Passages expressing regret over the passing of the landed Anglo-Irish gentry from Kerry dot the dialogue every so often. Because Mrs. Davenport dreams up the anagram, Ewn Andzale (for New Zealand), while working crossword puzzles, Howard Slaughter suggests that the plot of *The Coming of Ewn Andzale* is the result of Fitzmaurice's own fascination with crossword puzzles. During the last years of his life, he worked crossword puzzles, especially the Ximenes in the London *Observer*, while sitting in St. Stephen's Green, always on the same bench opposite the Russell Hotel.[2]

None of the ten plays discussed in this chapter are as good as the fantasies. They all have occasional flashes of inspiration but generally they exhibit a steady regression and even "an ominous note of self parody. It seems that before middle age, an unique but limited talent had expended itself." [3] But even the weakest plays are saved by snatches of brilliant dialogue.

CHAPTER 6

Assessment

NOT long before *The Country Dressmaker* was produced,
Yeats wrote, "a theatre such as we project should give a
reasonably complete expression to the imaginative interests of its
country. In any case, it was easier, and therefore wiser, to begin
where our art is most unlike that of others, with the representation of country life."[1] Lady Gregory shared Yeats' sentiments.
Consistently she saw the theater as part of the same movement
which had earlier given impetus to the Gaelic League:

> It was a movement for keeping the Irish language a spoken one, with, as
> a chief end, the preserving of our nationality. That does not sound like
> the beginning of a revolution, yet it was one. It was the discovery, the
> disclosure of folk-learning, the folk-poetry, the folk-tradition. Our
> Theatre was caught into the current, and it is that current, as I believe,
> that has brought it on its triumphant way. It is chiefly known now as
> folk-theatre. It has not only the great mass of primitive material and
> legend to draw on, but it has been made a living thing by the
> excitement of that discovery.[2]

All of George Fitzmaurice's work shows an abiding interest in
the folk. He is sympathetic with the Kerry people, for among
them he found the material for his plays. His dramatic figures,
very different from the stage Irishman, are dramatic representa-
tions of the reality he saw around him. The Kerry people are
peasants who live in solitude, inhibited by their religion, by their
folklore, even by their geography. And yet it is these same forces
which stimulated rather than inhibited Fitzmaurice. He was
entranced by the peculiarities of his fellow Kerrymen, and it is
this which brought authenticity and originality to his work.

Like Synge and Lady Gregory, Fitzmaurice attempted to
reproduce a particular dialect of western Ireland. Even so, many
words he used in his plays are derived directly from Gaelic and

are not found in the plays of the other two folk dramatists. Unlike Synge, who first studied Gaelic as an adult, Fitzmaurice came from a home in which Gaelic was a second language. Lady Gregory knew Gaelic, but she recorded an English dialect containing fewer words and idioms taken directly from the Irish. Writing at a time when interest in Anglo-Irish dialect was intense, Fitzmaurice demonstrated a remarkable ear for dialect literature. But he believed, along with Synge and Lady Gregory, that the sources for the new Irish Theatre should be in Irish peasant life as well as in Anglo-Irish language. Ireland, in his day, had rediscovered the imagination of the folk and he and Synge and Lady Gregory saw an untapped source in this folklore for the creation of an imaginative literature grounded in an almost broken tradition. It is in this sense that George Fitzmaurice, John Synge, and Augusta Gregory are folk dramatists.

As early as 1922, Ernest Boyd wrote that "George Fitzmaurice is . . . . the legitimate successor of Synge . . . . amongst the serious exponents of the folk play."[3] Seven years later Andrew Malone called Fitzmaurice "the one important folk dramatist whose work has been almost consistently ignored in Ireland, and yet remains unknown abroad."[4] In spite of such early claims about Fitzmaurice's importance as a folk dramatist, contemporary judgment of his talent is ambivalent, but can perhaps be understood in the context of the achievement of his fellow folk playwrights, Synge and Lady Gregory.

I *Comparison with Synge*

The tension between dream and actuality is central to both Synge and Fitzmaurice. This much used literary theme takes on a particular cast with each dramatist. In Fitzmaurice's plays, the tension is closely related to three recurrent motifs: that man must compromise his dream to survive, that the dreamer who will not compromise must stand apart in terrible solitude from his fellowmen, and that in upholding his lonely cause he becomes something of a fool. The figures in Fitzmaurice's best folk fantasies are driven by an impossible dream, a single-minded, intense longing, which gives them a vision of some good beyond the poverty or drabness or terror which surrounds them. Yet, characters like Leum, Jaymony, and Roger are nearly always frustrated because they refuse to compromise; hence the tragic undertones, the somberness pervading Fitzmaurice's work. We are forced to react to these "outsiders' ambivalently. Simultaneously we feel the forlorn estrangement they experience, while we understand that they themselves have deliberately kept aloof from reality. They cannot make any compromise which would lessen their self–imposed "exile." The noncompromiser for most Irish dramatists is nearly always a hero; he is a man of principle. Not for Fitzmaurice: the dreamers of his folk fantasies are unheroic and comic; they are ineffectual and, in the case of Jaymony and Roger are petty. Moreover, Leum and Jaymony and Roger are irresponsible; they live to create and to dream, ignoring domestic chores and family responsibility. Because they seek an unachievable perfection, they are fools.

In the more realistic plays the "heroes" and "heroines" are not fools precisely because they will compromise. The characters learn to be content with life as it is rather than as they would like it to be. Julia Shea, Dermot Rue Mullarkey, and Pete Munnix are forced by events to live with the realization that actuality never measures up to the dream. In writing about these figures, Fitzmaurice urges the stoic acceptance of what life has to offer. These antiheroic views are often wryly embodied in farce as in *'Twixt the Giltinans and the Carmodys* and *The Simple Hanrahans,* or in romantic comedy as in *The Country Dressmaker.* Luke Quilter expresses this bitter-comic dichotomy which results in Fitzmaurice's antiheroic vision of life. "I have the name of being a jolly man with no troubles on me, . . . and it's only a way I have for shaping through a mournful world."

Synge also depicts the noncompromiser, the hero who will not accept second best, and the fact that such a person is a hero or heroine for Synge accounts for a major difference between the two dramatists. The particular outlook Fitzmaurice brings to the tension between dream and reality is that one must compromise the dream and accept second best, namely, reality. Fitzmaurice's view is a nonglorified one—in contrast to Synge's.[5] Consider Synge's *Dierdre of the Sorrows.* In the play beautiful young Deirdre is destined from birth to fall in love with the handsome Naisi even though she had been promised to the High King of Ulster, Conchubor. Deirdre rejects Conchubor and elopes to Scotland with Naisi where they live for seven happy years. Deirdre and Naisi understand that death is an actuality overhanging love's dream, so they go back to Emain to face death rather than endure the agony of living with a dream they know must fade. The only way to defeat decay is to end life and love when they are starting to decline. Deirdre, like so many of Fitzmaurice's characters, is a noncompromiser, but certainly not a fool. Synge depicts the noncompromiser often, but such a person becomes noble and dignified and sometimes, as in the case of Deirdre, heroic, by not compromising. This is opposed to Fitzmaurice's view, and certainly accounts for the fact that there is none of the romance in Fitzmaurice's world that there is in Synge's.

Nowhere is this romance more pronounced than in *The Playboy.* When the villagers admire Christy for killing his father, he begins to dream of being somebody. His imagination then works upon the actuality, the weakling Christy has always been, until by the end of the play Christy actually becomes the playboy the villagers thought he was at first. Beyond any doubt, he demonstrates that he has the poet in him. Christy develops from a tongue-tied boy to a master of imaginative language. The villagers turn on him since they can no longer understand him, but the playboy has risen above the very people who nurtured his soul. The reality of what Christy knows himself to be in the first scene is transformed by his dream into a new reality, and in the end the dream and reality are one. Christy is a real hero after all, because he holds onto his dream, because he will not compromise. If he had been a Fitzmaurice figure, he would have become a fool and a failure, not only in Pegeen's and the villagers' eyes, but in his own. It is difficult to imagine Fitzmaurice accepting the belief that actuality could ever measure up to the ideal.

Different from *The Playboy* is *The Well of the Saints* where dream and reality are at complete variance. The main theme of the play is that naked actuality is intolerable. Mary and Martin Doul owe their comparative happiness to their acceptance of a belief which everyone, except them, knows is not based on facts, namely, that they are a grand, handsome couple. Shortly after the plays begins, they are faced with a hard reality when the Saint gives them sight, and they are frozen with the horror of their ugliness. Sight destroys the comforting fiction which made life bearable for them. After both are totally disillusioned, a new dream begins to take shape: Mary will become an old woman with "soft white hair" and Martin creates his own vision of himself with "a beautiful, long, white, silken streamy beard." When the new dream is firmly established, they are as happy as they were before the old one was shattered. They wholeheartedly renounce reality, for reality came close to destroying them. Here again we see the essentially different outlooks of the two dramatists. Synge shows in *The Well of the Saints* that people are sensible to blind themselves to a reality which torments them, and are pragmatic to protect and defend the vision that sustains their belief in their own human worth. Even though there is a deep grain of ironic satire in this as well as in other Synge comedies, and even though there is a dark streak of inner melancholy in Mary and Martin, as in his other peasants, Synge relishes the Douls' individualism. They are not compromisers, and they are not foolish, nor are they defeated. For all their comic vitality and longing, they are confronted with the cruelty of real life, so that their defiance of the saint is a perilous victory because it is a victory of the imagination. But it is a victory. Mary Doul calls herself the wonder of the western world, and so she is in her struggle to assert her dignity. Jaymony, a Fitzmaurice analogue to Martin and Mary, also tries to shut out reality. Not only does he fail, he is killed in the attempt. Significantly, one admires the Douls for their opposition to the Saint and to the villagers, while Jaymony is totally pathetic. Fitzmaurice's "heroes" are all so comically absurd. Though both Synge and Fitzmaurice embody a fund of folklore which they express in a style that retains the essential features of peasant speech, each has a sense of dream and a sense of reality which is antithetical to the other.

There is still another essential difference between the two folk dramatists, and that is their perception and consciousness of nature. Synge, for example, is filled with a deep awareness of the close connection between man and the natural world. Not only is the natural world the most prominent aspect of his imagery, but nature is often thematically essential to a play's total meaning. As the title implies, one of the most active forces of *In the Shadow of the Glen* is the surrounding countryside. This play is an excellent example of Synge's working upon material supplied by his environment, as the effect of that environment is felt throughout the play. People are obsessed by it. A kind of despondency hangs over them in the sense that the glen is a malevolent influence which affects everyone. Nora's complaint—"... for what good is a bit of a farm with cows on it, and sheep on the back hills, when you do be sitting looking out from a door the like of that door, and seeing nothing but the mists rolling down the bog, and the mists again, and they rolling up the bog, and hearing nothing but the wind crying out in the bits of broken trees were left from the great storm, and the streams roaring with the rain ..."—evokes the gloom and melancholy of the surroundings and, at the same time, is a metaphor for Nora's dismal life with Dan.

In *Riders to the Sea* nature is so much a part of the play that the sea could be called the antagonist. Throughout the short one act, there are recurring references to the predominance of the sea in the life of the islanders. Cathleen asks Nora, "Is the sea bad by the white rocks?" and is told "Middling bad, God help us. There is a great roaring in the west, and it's worse it'll be getting when the tide's turned to the wind." The points of the compass are used to emphasize the island-nature of the locale. Michael has been found in "the far north"; the wind is "rising from the south and west"; the mainland lies in the east; "the hooker's tacking from the east."

Specific images derived from the world of nature are strikingly absent from Fitzmaurice's drama. This is surprising because fifteen of seventeen plays are set in the wildest and most beautiful part of western Ireland. Synge was moved by this Kerry scenery as he tells us in his essay, "In West Kerry." Looking out over the sea he perceived "a splendour that was almost a grief to the mind." He seems to have been more deeply affected by the natural world than by anything else in Kerry, and the most noteworthy parts of his essay are molded round some description of natural scenery. Nearly every visitor to Kerry responds with the same enthusiasm. The Kerry environment is there for Fitzmaurice, too, but in a very different way. He grew up in "that wild place away in the mountains,"[6] and he understood that the mists that continually rise from the Stacks Mountains made the people superstitious, perhaps more so than the peasants from other parts of western Ireland. Jamesie Kennelly invoked the Linnaun Shee "in the glens and the haunted places"; the Grey Man tells Cauth he came "pout of a briny spot, then, a place where periwinkles are plenty, and there is dilisk thrown in heaps" on a haunted eve of May. Fitzmaurice knew that the remoteness of the area made the peasants insular and suspicious:

Indeed, 'tis tired enough I am of them and praising them, the ears cocked by them and they suspicious, in a manner you'd have to consider before letting the silliest word out of your mouth if you wouldn't find yourself in middle of a revolt and a hillabilloo.[7]

... the generality of the ... [Kerry] people are nothing short of being a pack of the biggest theives, rogues, and robbers, diddling each other at fairs over horses with blind eyes, cows with paralysed udders, and so on in the line of blemishes.[8]

Like Gaugin who did not actually paint the Tahitian landscape, but who conveyed its beauty via rich, warm color, so too Fitzmaurice did not use Kerry's splendor as the basis of his imagery, but wrote of it indirectly, of its influence on its inhabitants. He absorbed and recreated the visual world in terms of emotional color. The Grey Man is a "hoary man of the ocean," and Donal Bluebeard lives on Dhoul-na-Ferris, "a miserable spot of rocks and bushes," in the "fearsome" Bay of Doon. Fitzmaurice understood how frightening the sea can be when it "is roaring in the wild and dreary nights." And he understood the greedy tyranny of the land, not only in the respect that peasants' lives were built on the hard reality of uneconomic holdings, but also in the respect that the constantly changing weather and light cause vagaries of personality. It is no accident that Luke Quilter and Morgan Quille are "mountainy men." Because of the ironic critical stance Fitzmaurice takes toward these peasants, his plays reek of cowdung and Kerry insularity. So what Fitzmaurice "gets at" through the wildness and the unpredictability of the sea and mists of his native landscape is that his characters are constricted by an environmental experience which they fear to enlarge.

II   *Comparison with Lady Gregory*

Though Synge and Fitzmaurice are both folk dramatists, they obviously handle folk materials and environment very differently. Lady Gregory's plays are also based on the folk mind and folk speech, and she too is different from Fitzmaurice. For one thing, Lady Gregory's world includes a variety of characters not associated with Fitzmaurice. Her characters are commonly lumped under the heading of peasant, but in fact many of them are peasant only in the sense of not being "Ascendancy"; they have a much wider social range than the characters of Fitzmaurice. To take one play, *Hyacinth Halvey*, there is Hyacinth, a small town official, Mrs. Delane, the postmistress, James Quirke, a butcher, a priest's housekeeper, a police sergeant, a telegraph boy. Any one of these people would be affronted if taken for a tiller of the soil. Besides an occasional priest, a butcher from *The Terrible Baisht*, and a national teacher from *The Simple Hanrahans*, all the people of Fitzmaurice's fifteen Kerry plays are farmers. As Morgan Quille asks, "Isn't all the world born farmers?" Lady Gregory, on the other hand, writes of all kinds of people, people like Bartley Fallon, the henpecked little man of *Spreading the News*, who takes a lugubrious joy in his own misfortunes; like Peggy Mahon, the old midwife and Thomas Coppinger, the stone cutter from *The Image*; like the artist in *McDonough's Wife*; and like the rich farmer, Nicholas, in *Dave*. And besides characters from her folk comedies, Lady Gregory wrote folk histories about the tragic heroines of Irish history, Gormleith, Dervorgilla, and Grania. Such a variety of occupation and class is not part of Fitzmaurice's ken. Julia Shea, Peter Guerin, Leum O'Donoghue, Padden Shanahan, and even Luke Quilter and Morgan Quille, are poor, struggling Kerry farmers. Thus, Lady Gregory and Fitzmaurice differ greatly in the people they write about: Lady Gregory's plays are essentially intimate and affectionate glimpses into many facets of Irish life, while George Fitzmaurice's plays depict narrowly drawn personalities nearly all of whom are small farmers.

But what most sets Lady Gregory and Synge apart from George Fitzmaurice is that they are chiefly concerned with giving expression to the universals of the human experience by means of the particular Irish experience, whereas Fitzmaurice's main concern is to show that particular Irish peasant experience. Fitzmaurice left no pronouncements concerning the aim of his drama, but his thematic practices suggest that he was not interested in seeking a more universal reference.

Fitzmaurice pictures a peasant reality which defeats any possible dream. The peasant-idealist is opposed by members of his own family, by the power of the church, and by superstitions of his native culture—the enemy within. Fitzmaurice's whole antiheroical vision of life is dramatized by means of Kerry matchmaking and hunger for land. He is content to express this rural experience in a way it had never been done before. But for Synge, the Irish folk experience is a means for expressing larger truths.

Consider *Riders to the Sea* in which Maurya, who has already lost a husband and five sons to the sea, is helpless to prevent her sixth and last son, Bartley, from going to his death on his way to the mainland from his Aran Island home. Though the play opens in the everyday world with Cathleen kneading a cake, *Riders to the Sea* has universal implications. Though the play is grounded in Irish folklore and Irish rural life, there is a mythic quality about it as well. One of Maurya's possessions is a pig with black feet; pigs in Irish mythology are thought to belong to the Other World. There is reference to "the black hags that do be flying on the sea." The "ghost horse" emphasizes this world of specter and spirit, as does Maurya's apparition of Michael riding a grey pony. The very title is mythic: we are all riders to the sea, for as Maurya tells us, "no man can be living forever." Maurya's lament begins as a keen for Bartley and Michael, then it moves on to an expression of sorrow for all her family, for all the islanders, and finally, for all humanity who must face a hostile universe. George Fitzmaurice's plays are grounded in the same folklore and rural life which Synge appropriated for his drama, but his nonidealization of the supernatural subverts any possible mythic interpretation on the part of his readers.

In addition to these mythic intimations, *Riders to the Sea* is very like Greek tragedy. The climax occurs offstage; forebodings are voiced throughout the one act; the keening women are reminiscent of the chorus; and the pervasive dramatic irony is much like that of Greek tragedy. Bartley's farewell speech is just one example of this irony: "I'll have half an hour to go down, and you'll see me coming again, in two days, or in three days, or maybe in four days if the wind is bad." The point is, he does come home again, but as a corpse.

It would be absurd to look at *Riders* as of strictly regional interest. The island is Aran and its predicaments are those of the islanders. Though Synge portrayed the profound sadness and dignity of the Aran peasant, he also meant to depict a life which he felt revealed the essence of all of Ireland. When most local, he sought to express the national, the universal, the mythic. He tried to show how Ireland herself could develop her awareness of the universal elements of the human condition by studying the life on these peasants. Synge reverses the process from the particular to the universal in *In the Shadow of the Glen,* where he uses an ageless story found in various forms on several continents, a tale that sets up an "eternal" situation—the triangle of husband, wife, and lover, and adroitly fuses into the tale, without losing the universality of the original, the Irish rural experience of the loveless marriage.

Fitzmaurice sought only to dramatize the Irish rural experience. *The Country Dressmaker* is not a play about "courting"; it is about the very specific and local matchmaking conventions George Fitzmaurice knew from firsthand experience. *The Ointment Blue* and *The Enchanted Land* portray "folk royalty," not actual kingship. Even though it is possible to find some universal implication in all literature, Fitzmaurice, unlike Synge, is not interested in going beyond his Irish material to make analogous statements about life in general; he is content to express his view of things within the context of the Kerry peasant life he knew best. It is probably safe to say that his view of things is a direct outgrowth of his observations of this life.

The base of Lady Gregory's theater was the Galway area around Coole Park. She expressed her comic vision by reproducing the county dialect she heard almost daily and by portraying the people among whom she lived. Like Synge she used the particular Irish experience in order to make observations about life in general. For instance, in *Spreading the News* she is laughing at her characters, but she is laughing at what is universal in them, not only at what is accidental or "peasant." She is not only satirizing the Irish talent for exaggeration, but the fact that we all relish a scandal. The point is, the credulous market folk of *Spreading the News* have their counterparts everywhere. This same statement could not be applied to Fitzmaurice's characters. Luke Quilter and Morgan Quille, the mountainy men, Malachi Cantillon, the gombeen man, Keerby, the priest's fearful clerk, are types indigenous to the west of Ireland.

It is known that Lady Gregory meant to universalize: she recognized the university of the themes which appealed to her and then wrote of them within the framework of Kiltartan. Her notes accompanying *The Wrens* describe this process: "Some-

times in making a plan for a play I set the scene in some other
country that I may be sure the emotion displayed is not bounded
by any neighborhood but is a unversal one.[9] A good example is
The Gaol Gate in which three boys from a mountain village have
been arrested for murder. Rumor has spread that Denis has
informed against Terry (who really is guilty) in order to be freed.
Young Mary, Denis' wife, only wants to have Denis free, but old
Mary, though she loves her son, thinks a good name is more
important than life. The two women learn that Denis did not
inform and that he has been hanged, although he is innocent. The
young woman is overwhelmed with grief, but for the old one it is
a triumph that her son was no informer. They typify eternally
contrasted attitudes: the pragmatic versus the idealistic. Even
though "informing" has special meaning in Ireland, the chief
point of the drama is not dependent on its locale.

III   *The Nationality of Fitzmaurice*

More than anything else, it is the universality of Synge and
Lady Gregory as opposed to the "nationality" of Fitzmaurice
which sets up the contrast between them. Great drama rises
above its locale and time; Synge's and Lady Gregory's plays
transcend Wicklow and Kiltartan. They adapted native tales to
traditional dramatic form. That they did this well is shown by
their rank as European dramatists.

But Synge and Lady Gregory are writing about a life they have
not lived, though they write of it with compassion and love. The
beginnings of Synge's intimate knowledge of the Irish peasant,
for example, came in 1898 when he visited the Aran Islands (off
the coat of Galway) for the first time. Elizabeth Coxhead
describes the effects of that trip in her book *J. M. Synge and
Lady Gregory.*

The knowledge he had been subconsciously acquiring during his fallow
years suddenly came into focus; he looked at these primitive people,
and through them into the heart of humanity. He found an almost
untouched peasant culture, with Irish as the universal language, and
with an extraordinary beauty and dignity in the bare cottages, the
women's red dresses and the men's grey homespuns against the creamy
limestone, the treasure of poems and the stories that beguiled the
evenings by the light of tiny cod-oil lamps. The chief industry was
fishing from curraghs, or canoes of lath and canvas, and in the wild seas

fatalities were frequent, so that men lived under the shadow of death, and women of bereavement; this bred in the people the passionate intensity of feeling for which the dramatist in Synge instinctively longed.

For five summers in succession he returned to the islands, living among the people as one of themselves, amusing them with conjuring tricks, absorbing their wildness and their strength.[10]

Most of the material for his plays came from his visits to Aran.

Lady Gregory, whose aristocratic origins were similar to Synge's, heard folk tales as a child from her governess. Moreover, she visited the peasants on her father's estate and helped them write letters to their children in America. This is how she gained her accurate insight into the peasant character. It was not until she was well into her forties that she learned Gaelic in order to be able to translate the peasants' tales into English. "This beginning of knowledge was a great excitement for me, for though I had heard all my life some talk of the fairies and the banshee, I had never thought of giving heed to what I, in common with my class, looked on as fancy or superstition."[11]

Lady Gregory and Synge write of the folk experience as spectators. Fitzmaurice, on the other hand, writes as if he were a peasant himself, though admittedly an ironic-critical one. He writes from the inside, as a participant. The Irish rural experience is the whole of life for Fitzmaurice, and because of this, what he does extremely well is to shape a fragment of life. Lacking the poetry and the hauntingly beautiful nature mysticism of Synge's plays and the classical structure of Lady Gregory's plays, Fitzmaurice's drama nevertheless presents the humor and pathos of Irish peasant life with vigor and a certain whimsical charm. The excellence of his plays has been overshadowed in part by the genius of Synge and Lady Gregory, whose plays have a stature that far exceeds the narrow boundaries of national drama.

Although George Fitzmaurice has limited himself to writing about peasant farm life, this life is a major part of the Irish national scene. Moreover, Ireland is a country where dreams are continually brutalized by reality, and Fitzmaurice appropriated this as the major theme of his work. Coexistence of the romantic ideal and harsh reality ends up for Fitzmaurice in the undermining of the ideal. Because the dream has little chance to grow in Kerry, there is none of the romance which exists in Lady

Gregory's and Synge's world to be found in George Fitzmaurice's drama. He is certainly the most authentic of the folk dramatists, and for this reason, as well as for his technical experimentation, he deserves some measure of the recognition enjoyed by his fellow folk dramatists, Synge and Lady Gregory.

CHAPTER 7

William Butler Yeats and the Obscurity of George Fitzmaurice

I   The Charges

IN 1963, in an obituary on George Fitzmaurice, Austin Clarke wrote "that the two Abbey directors [Yeats and Lady Gregory] deliberately kept Fitzmaurice off the stage as they feared to be overtaken by him as they had already been overtaken by Synge."[1] Again, in the introduction to George Fitzmaurice's *Fantasies*, Clarke claimed the playwright had discovered what Yeats and Lady Gregory were looking for—a way of creating a dramatic art form that could recreate and interpret the traditional Irish folklore—but because *The Magic Glasses* was more praised than works by Yeats and Lady Gregory when the company performed it in London, it was dropped from the repertoire.

Reading *The Dandy Dolls*, I wondered how Lady Gregory and Yeats could have failed to recognize the energy, vehement rhythm and imaginative originality of its two short acts, especially when they had already been pleased by *The Magic Glasses*. I was much puzzled by their rejection of the play and then a strange thought flashed into my mind. I happened to be in London at the time and I went straight to the Periodical Room of the British Museum and looked up in the dusty files the press notices of *The Magic Glasses* when it was brought to London by the Abbey Company. My unworthy suspicion proved right. A. B. Walkley had praised the play as the best in a small repertorie, which included plays by Yeats and Lady Gregory. Other leading dramatic critics were as enthusiastic. After that, *The Magic Glasses* disappeared from the Abbey stage.

Probably owing to Austin Clarke's prestige, more credence has been given his allegation than should be.

131

Irving Wardle in an article in *The London Magazine* in 1965 endorses Clarke's charges and gives added weight to them by quoting a statement Padraic Colum made in 1964: "We should have forced Yeats and Lady Gregory to accept Fitzmaurice as they forced Dublin to accept Synge."

In his dissertation on Fitzmaurice, Howard K. Slaughter agrees with Clarke and Colum, and then carries the charge even further. Because *The Country Dressmaker* was enthusiastically received by Dublin audiences, and because Yeats never experienced a like popularity, Slaughter concludes that Yeats was jealous of Fitzmaurice. Slaughter says more along these lines in the dissertation, in an article which appeared in *The Educational Theatre Journal,* and in the recently published book, *George Fitzmaurice and His Enchanted Land.*

Maurice Kennedy in Irish Writing (No. 15, p. 38) reports a story he had heard concerning an argument between Fitzmaurice and Yeats over the cutting of a line of dialogue. Synge would allow no cuts to his *Playboy* and Fitzmaurice followed his example. The enmity between Yeats and Fitzmaurice was deeper, perhaps, than anyone has ever recorded. Synge, however, had eclipsed Yeats and Lady Gregory in gaining fame as a playwright and perhaps, as Austin Clarke suggested many years later in his tribute to Fitzmaurice (*The Irish Press,* May 22, 1963, p. 8) they were afraid of being surpassed again.[2]

Catherine Rynne in an article in *The Story of the Abbey*[3] writes that Padraic Colum repeated Clarke's allegation, but this is not accurate. As Irving Wardle pointed out, Colum said nothing about Yeats' jealousy of Fitzmaurice, only that others who surrounded Yeats and Lady Gregory should have stood up for and defended Fitzmaurice's potential as a dramatist. Miss Rynne further claims that Colum told her that Yeats felt true peasant dialogue could only be written by one man, Synge, and he was therefore inclined to disregard anyone else with this ability. This may be perfectly true, but what it says is that Yeats disliked Fitzmaurice for not being Synge, and not because of jealousy.

On September 1, 1969, Hugh Hunt in *What's On: A Weekly Diary of the Arts* wrote: "I came across the play [*The Dandy Dolls*] recently when the Fitzmaurice collection was sent me for review. ... The power of its fantasy and its extraordinary imagery simply bowl you over. When the Abbey asked me to do 'The Well of the Saints' this summer, I decided I simply had to have 'The Dandy Dolls' as the curtain raiser. How Yeats and Lady Gregory could have turned it down I can't understand—unless perhaps it was *too good.*"

More recently, Mr. John Conbère in an article in *EIRE–Ireland* has repeated all the charges growing out of Austin Clarke's original statement, and comes to the conclusion that

> There is a fallacy in Mr. Clarke's argument, if this may be called 'an argument'. He based his suspicion on English reviews. As is illustrated in *The Irish Independent* review, the Irish critics were antagonistic toward *The Magic Glasses.* This difference of opinion between English and Irish critics was evident with respect to *The Pie-Dish* also. . . . But the *London Times'* reviewer gives the play lavish praise. . . . From the insight exhibited by the reviewer's remarks, it is clear he has done what the Irish critics could not do. He has approached the play with an open mind and grasped Fitzmaurice's artistic vision. Seeing that this difference of opinion is divided on national lines, it is not surprising to find Yeats siding with those who find Fitzmaurice's plays to be merely crude and frivolous. To judge Yeats' rejection solely on the English reviews, as Mr. Clarke seems to have done, renders too harsh a judgement.[4]

Again, it is true that the Irish reviewers did not like Fitzmaurice. In the case of *The Pie-Dish*, they did not understand the play; nor for that matter did the English reviewers. However, the English critics were impressed by whatever it was Fitzmaurice was trying to do, whereas the Irish journalists saw only what they took to be slurs on the national character. There is no doubt that the Irish reviewers took offense because they felt Fitzmaurice was making fun of them, as well as of the Irish peasant. It is not true that it is *not* surprising to find Yeats siding with Irish journalists. All one has to do is to go through various newspapers and journals of this time and he will find numberless examples of Yeats' open warfare with the press. In a letter he wrote in 1907, for example: "We have had another performance of *The Country Dressmaker* since I wrote, and the success was greater than before. The dear *Freeman,* or rather its evening issue which is called by another name, has congratulated us on having got a play at last 'to which nobody can take the slightest exception' or some such words." And again, in the same letter: "The principal actors are now applauded at their entrances with a heartiness unknown before, and both Lady Gregory and myself received several times last spring what newspaper writers call 'an ovation.'"[5] These statements reveal the scorn Yeats often felt for the Irish reviewers of Abbey performances.

At any rate, to refute Austin Clarke's imputation of Yeats' jealousy by citing the difference between Irish and English reviewers is to sidestep the issue. The question is: did Yeats deliberately force Fitzmaurice into obscurity because he was envious of a potential rival? The answer is positively and categorically, No.

II   *In Defense of Yeats*

To begin with, Yeats did not like *The Country Dressmaker* at first, and it is only owing to chance that it was produced at all. An excerpt from Joseph Holloway's diary explains: "He [Fitzmaurice] was surprised when I told him I thought his play would have never been accepted, only Boyle withdrew his work, and the company was in a hole."[6] What Holloway is talking about is Boyle's reaction to *The Playboy* riots. Shortly after the most tumultuous event in Dublin theatrical history, *The Playboy* premiere, William Boyle wrote to *The Freeman's Journal* publicly dissociating himself from the Abbey Theatre and withdrawing his three plays from its repertoire. Even though Yeats had a low opinion of Boyle's writing, his three plays had been popular and their loss was a blow. Immediately after *The Playboy* had finished its run, Willie Fay went to London to reason with Boyle, but with no luck. It was eighteen months before Boyle came back to the fold and five years before he gave the Abbey a new play.

It was obvious that *The Country Dressmaker* was produced only because of Boyle's action. Probably Fitzmaurice's play, at least in Yeats' and Lady Gregory's judgment, was the best available, and a play was needed desperately if the Abbey was not to fold. It is the more ironical then, that the unwanted drama was a huge popular success.

After its premiere, Yeats wrote in a letter to John Quinn, that he did not like the play, but admired its sincerity. After the second performance he was even more amazed at its success, but was delighted, saying he intended to put the play on again the following week owing to its attraction. In the same letter he expressed the opinion that "Fitzmaurice ... wrote it with the special object of showing up the sordid side of country life. He thinks himself a follower of Synge, which he is not. I have no doubt that there will be enthusiasm tonight, and that the author, who has been thirsting for the crown of martyrdom will be called before the curtain for the third night running.["]7 Yeats is simply saying he thinks Fitzmaurice a poor imitator of Synge. This is, no doubt, the reason for the rather unjust "who has been thirsting for the crown of martyrdom." Since Synge was repudiated by the Dublin public for his honesty in portraying the Irish peasant, then, reasons Yeats, Fitzmaurice will want the same adverse publicity. The same faulty reasoning is operative when Slaughter affirms that because Synge would allow no cuts in dialogue, neither would Fitzmaurice.[8] Yeats and Slaughter are not the only ones to think Fitzmaurice a follower of Synge. Joseph Holloway wrote:

I was introduced to young Fitzmaurice, the writer of *The Country Dressmaker*, and found him a nice, unassuming fellow with, I am sorry to say, a hankering after Synge and his methods of presenting the Irish character on the boards. We had a long argument over the matter, but he was of the same opinion at the end, I fear. He thinks hardly of the Irish peasant, but agreed that the stage was a place for selection, and everything one saw or heard should not be crudely noted down and served up for the townsfolk's consumption. Much of peasants' ways would seem hard and coarse and be misunderstood by audiences in the Abbey, for instance. I like Fitzmaurice and hope he won't be spoiled by the cult.[9]

Fitzmaurice obviously disagreed with Yeats' and Holloways's judgment that he was copying Synge ("we had a long argument over the matter"), but because he wrote in dialect and because he depicted rural life starkly, he was thought to be a hanger on of the "cult."

The only other direct evidence of Yeats' awareness of George Fitzmaurice is a part of a postscript to a letter written to Lady Gregory in 1913: "I saw the last act and half of *The Country Dressmaker* last night. I wasn't very well—journey over has upset me—and had stayed away expecting to be bored. I wish now I had seen the whole, it was astonishingly good.[10]

It is obvious Yeats changed his opinion about *The Country Dressmaker*. But even if he had not, the play had already been revived several times. Is it probable that a jealous man would allow the work of a potential rival to be performed so frequently? Since Yeats was a director, and in fact it would be no exaggeration to say *the* director of the Abbey, if the play was performed, it was with Yeats' knowledge and authorization.

Probably because of *The Country Dressmaker's* success, *The Pie-Dish* and *The Magic Glasses* were performed. Both plays were exceedingly unpopular and misunderstood. Not long after *The Magic Glasses* was produced, *The Dandy Dolls* was rejected. Even though, as John Conbere has pointed out in his article in *EIRE–Ireland*, Yeats could not have liked Fitzmaurice because their outlooks were essentially opposed, in that Yeats romanticized Ireland's legendary past whereas Fitzmaurice's view of things was a nonglorified one, Yeats was willing to stage a play like *The Magic Glasses* and even to take it on tour in England— and this despite the very bad Irish reviews. Fitzmaurice's antiromantic outlook is especially blatant in *The Dandy Dolls*, for even the supernatural is antiheroic; yet even so, this cannot explain Yeats' refusal to stage the play, for he himself in several very early poems, like "The Stolen Child," "The Hosting of the Sidhe," and "The Happy Townland," all published before *The Dandy Dolls*, perceived more and more the very dangers of the fairy world which Fitzmaurice was illuminating. Both men understood the attraction and the danger inherent in the supernatural fairyland; they both knew the supernatural afforded escape from the pallid everydayness of life, while at the same time exerted a constricting hold on those who believed in the fairy world.

Whether Yeats did or did not, would or would not appreciate Fitzmaurice's fantasies is not relevant to his rejection of *The Dandy Dolls*. Yeats could not tolerate William Boyle's plays, but he produced them because they were popular. If *The Pie-Dish* and *The Magic Glasses* had been well received, *The Dandy Dolls* most likely would have been performed. Concerning Yeats' jealousy of Fitzmaurice, Michael Oh Aodha has written in (*The Journal of Irish Literature* in May, 1972) that

It is an interesting but implausible theory. Yeats seldom got enthusiastic notices for his plays at home or abroad in those years; but this never influenced him in providing a stage for worthwhile work or from championing the cause of any dramatist whose work he admired. Lady Gregory's help and kindness to other writers was unstinting.

A more likely explanation is that Fitzmaurice was uncertain and thinskinned in the face of harsh Dublin criticism. He had neither the inclination nor the temperament to stand in the limelight. He had, in fact, an inordinate fear of critics and the attendant publicity. On one occasion, he allowed the Abbey actor, Eamon Kelly to stage an amateur production of *The Country Dressmaker* in Dagg Hall on the strict understanding that no critics would be invited. On another occasion when a radio production of *The Magic Glasses*, recorded in the authentic dialect of his native district, was planned, he would not allow a broadcast. When his Kerry neighbour and fellow-playwright, Bryan MacMahon, tried to honor him in his native Listowel, George first hid from him and then went literally 'on the run.'

To blame Fitzmaurice's present day obscurity on Yeats' jealousy of a potential rival is false.

III   *Back to Austin Clarke*

Why, then, would an eminent poet and playwright like Austin Clarke make such a charge? Could it be because Yeats did not include Austin Clarke in *The Oxford Book of Modern Verse* which he compiled in 1935? Undoubtedly this exclusion bothered Clarke, but he should have taken consolation in the sensation the anthology caused when it appeared in 1936, a sensation because Yeats' prejudices are so blatantly obvious. Among other things, Yeats favors his friends' poetry. Verses of Margot Ruddock, Dorothy Wellesley, and the Swami (Shri Purohit Swami) keep company with those of C. Day Lewis, D. H. Lawrence, and A. E. Housman. In the preface Yeats refers to Oliver St. John Gogarty as "one of the great lyric poets of the age." Granted that Gogarty may have been one of the wittiest of men, he was certainly not one of most lyric. Gogarty was a skilled surgeon, an aviator, a senator, a playwright, a champion athlete, but not "one of the great lyric poets of the age." There were seventeen of Gogarty's poems included in the anthology, almost twice as many as those of any other poet in the book. Obviously Austin Clarke was not Yeats' friend. Could this have bothered him? Vindictiveness may or may not have been a motive in what Clarke said about Yeats' rejection of *The Dandy Dolls.* We will never know. At any rate, Clarke will never lack sympathetic listeners to his Fitzmaurice theory, for the number of commentators calling attention of Yeats' supposed jealousy is legion.

Anthony Butler, for example, wrote an article for *The Story of the Abbey Theatre*[11] to show the "conniving ego" of Yeats, and "selfishness ... meanness and ... unscrupulous intrigues" of Yeats, and how he wanted no rival to his fame. Again, Herbert Howarth in *The Irish Writers*[12] points out that the poet was jealous of every near rival and that Yeats was so anxious that the Irish literary movement should be remembered as *his* movement that he sometimes altered facts in this direction.

Thus, it is hard to squelch this petty accusation. Perhaps quoting pertinent sections of Sean O'Casey's *Inishfallen, Fare Thee Well* will help put things in a proper perspective.

Some in Dublin hated Yeats, official Catholics feared him, and a group of younger writers disliked his booming opinions on literature. ... A number of these last, headed by F. R. Higgins, the poet, Liam O'Flaherty and Brinsley Macnamara, the novelists, and Cecil Salkeld, the young painter, had started a Radical Club to nourish the thoughts and ambitions of the young writers, in opposition to the elderly and wild spectulations of Yeats and the adulatory group that trailed longingly after him. Some of these wanted to hook in Sean so that his newer influence might be useful in putting Yeats in his improper place. ... Sean, however, had no bubbling desire to be O'Flaherty's gillie, ... for he saw clearly enough that O'Flaherty in the way of arrogance and sense of being a superior being, was worse than Yeats without the elder man's grace and goodwill.[13]

O'Casey goes on to say he had to pay for his refusal to join the campaign to make Yeats a little humbler. When his next play, *Juno and the Paycock*, appeared at the Abbey, Higgins wrote a very nasty letter condemning it to *The Irish Statesman*. "Austin Clarke, the poet, joined in the fight, gently, but none the less bitterly, indicative of what he thought about the play, saying 'The Playwright seemed to be trying to exploit the poor!'"[14]

Again, when *The Plough and the Stars* was given at the Abbey, "the intellectuals [especially bitter in their attacks were O'Flaherty, Higgins, and Clarke] began to send letters to the press, and to A E's [George Russell] journal, *The Irish Statesman*. Some of them were influenced to do this, Sean thought, because he had definitely refused to join them in a Club or Society which was to be organized to put the arrogant Yeats in his place." O'Casey said he would defy Yeats when he thought he should, "but he wouldn't join any clique to do it, because he thought this opposition was born of envy of the great fame the poet enjoyed as the leading man of Irish letters."[15]

Sean O'Casey tells us he was shocked "to watch this mean and reprehensible envy of the poet's literary standing bubbling up in the minds of educated and cultured, but lesser men."[16] Significantly, O'Casey wrote all this long after *The Silver Tassie* controversy;[17] his defense of Yeats, then, is all the most impressive.

To sum up, it is impossible to say with any certainty why Austin Clarke accused Yeats of jealousy in regard to George Fitzmaurice. Obviously he was not alone in thinking so. The allegation is rash and foolish, and once having put it out of sight, we can thank Mr. Clarke for rescuing such an interesting playwright from an undeserved obscurity.

CHAPTER 8

Conclusion

I Overall Reputation

BY birth an outsider, by personality a loner, it is not surprising that Fitzmaurice was neglected in a gossipy, competitive, literary place like Dublin. Only because his first play, *The Country Dressmaker*, was so popular did the Abbey produce *The Pie-Dish* and *The Magic Glasses*, neither of which was liked by Dublin audiences. No one paid much attention to George Fitzmaurice until the fall of 1914 when the publishing house of Maunsel brought out *Five Plays* which included the three already produced by the Abbey and two it had rejected: *The Dandy Dolls* and *The Moonlighter*. Ernest Boyd, in his well received *Ireland's Literary Renaissance* (1916), called *Five Plays* the best thing to happen to Irish drama since the death of Synge, an assessment which prompted the Abbey to put on another Fitzmaurice play, *'Twixt the Giltinans and the Carmodys*. In the next two years the playwright published two plays in *The Dublin Magazine*. Then in 1929 his plays were reviewed favorably by Andrew Malone in his literary history of *The Irish Drama*.

Such critical successes may have heartened Fitzmaurice, but they were too few to assure his reputation. Imagine his surprise, then, when he was chosen as one of the best writers in Ireland between 1900 and '1930. The Irish government commissioned artist Harry E. Clarke to produce a stained glass window depicting scenes from the work of fifteen writers. Three-quarters of the bottom left panel of the window, now at the Municipal Gallery of Modern Art in Dublin, is a representation of Jaymony from *The Magic Glasses*. Fragments of red, purple, and gold glass form the figure of the young peasant who is gazing at several glasses floating before him, below which is the inscription: "It's the pleasure and diversion of the world you'll hear and see in the magic glasses."

In spite of such unexpected recognition, between 1930 and 1940, Fitzmaurice seems to have discontinued writing. No play had appeared on the Abbey stage since 1923, nor in *The Dublin Magazine* since 1926. Then, out of the blue, a review of his work appeared in *The Dublin Magazine* in 1940 by the distinguished poet, Austin Clarke. It was the fantasies which impressed Clarke, so he sought out the playwright for permission to produce one. Fearing the newspapers critics' reaction to his work, Fitzmaurice repeatedly refused his consent. Finally, thanks to Clarke's gentle persistance, *The Dandy Dolls* were presented by the Lyric Theatre Group in 1945. This production sparked new interest in the neglected dramatist. In 1948 Liam Miller, publisher of the Dolmen Press, staged *The Moonlighter* and in 1949 Clarke put on *The Linnaun Shee*.

His belated discovery did nothing to change Fitzmaurice's reclusive behavior. Bryan MacMahon, a fellow Kerry playwright, tried to obtain permission to perform *The Magic Glasses* at the Listowel Drama Festival. He was turned down. MacMahon tried again, the second time writing a letter to Fitzmaurice, inviting him to return to Listowel to be honored at a banquet and at a production of any one of his plays. He never received a reply. Not ready to give up, MacMahon applied for permission from the editor of the Talbot Press which had once published *The Magic Glasses* in a single copy. At long last, the Listowel Group presented *The Magic Glasses* which won the All-Ireland Prize at Athlone in 1951. Michael O'h Aodha of Radio Eireann recorded the production in order to play it over the air, but Fitzmaurice would not give his consent. Eamon Kelly, knowing how difficult or impossible it was to get the playwright's confidence, put on *The Dandy Dolls* in Dublin without trying to obtain an official permission. Hearing about rehearsals, the playwright was indignant and demanded that production cease. He finally relented when he was assured that no newspaper men would be allowed to review the play. Was there ever a writer who so consistently sacrificed his own work? Even so, critics continued to appreciate him; J. D. Riley and Maurice Kennedy published evaluations of his work in the 1950s and Seumas O'Sullivan, publisher of *The Dublin Magazine*, printed two more plays.

Not long before Fitzmaurice died, Bryan MacMahon confessed to him that he had put on *The Magic Glasses* without permission, and that the play had won Ireland's most prestigious drama award. MacMahon told the playwright that everyone in Kerry was proud of him for immortalizing such characters as Jaymony and Quille and for reproducing their speech so authentically. "Fitzmaurice's eyes misted over and he turned and said: 'Well, that's something, anyway.' "[1]

In spite of his reluctance to encourage any kind of acceptance, Fitzmaurice has achieved some renown. He has always been appreciated in Ireland by the literary establishment, and thanks to its refusal to let his work die, his plays are regularly staged in Dublin today. Two American scholars, Howard Slaughter and Robert Hogan have introduced Fitzmaurice's work to America. But it was never scholars nor literary men whom Fitzmaurice avoided; it was fear of and contempt for the popular press and the Dublin public that caused Fitzmaurice to shun production of his work. That *The Pie-Dish* and *The Magic Glasses* were so ill-received by the press and so misunderstood by the public obviously rankled over the years. Playgoers wanted sentimentality not truth, and Fitzmaurice would not give them what they wanted.

II   *In Defense of Nonsentimental Drama*

The following passage refers directly to Synge's *The Playboy of the Western World*, in which Christy Mahon tells some Mayo villagers that he has killed his father, thus becoming for this brave deed, a hero in their eyes; but it also refers indirectly to all peasant drama in which life is presented honestly:

"They do be putting quare plays on in Dublin nowadays! . . . Very quare plays. They do be putting on plays where a boy from the country kills his da!"
"That seems wrong."
"Yes. And they make us out to be nothing but cutthroats, and murderers, and dijinerates."
"What on earth do they mean by doing that?"
"They calls it—Art."[2]

These peasant plays, rooted in the soil and speech of Ireland, were concerned with revealing a life that had never been dramatized before. Despite their excellence, they were viewed with suspicion and distrust by the average Dubliner. In his plays, George Fitzmaurice portrays with uncomprising honesty one kind of man, the dairy farmer struggling to eke out his living in

North Kerry, and in fashioning this fragment of Irish experience he chooses unerringly what is fundamental in the manners and motives of these peasants. "The harshness of Fitzmaurice's world," writes Ann Saddlemyer, "is reflected in his comedy, his characters, and their language. Laughter is rough in a peasant world blackly etched in strong passions and words. Powerful personalities are crudely drawn, in keeping with the stark tragicomic situations through which they stride."[3] Fitzmaurice stubbornly opposed any softening of his work in order to make it more palatable to the Dublin playgoing public.

Yeats always defended the artist's right to present bitter unwelcome truths. In a speech before a 1907 audience of *The Playboy*, after several performances which had caused riots, Yeats said:

We have put this play before you to be heard and to be judged, as every play should be heard and judged. Every man has a right to hear it and condemn it if he pleases, but no man has a right to interfere with another man hearing a play and judging for himself. The country that condescends either to bully or to permit itself to be bullied soon ceases to have any fine qualities, and I promise you that if there is any small section in this theatre that wish to deny the right of others to hear what they themselves don't want to hear we will play on, and our patience shall last longer than their patience.[4]

Nineteen years later, in 1926, Yeats once again asserted the artist's right to be heard. Storming onto the stage on the first night of Sean O'Casey's *The Plough and the Stars*, he shouted, "You have disgraced yourselves again. Is this to be an ever-recurring celebration of the arrival of Irish genius? Once more you have rocked the cradle of genius. The news of what is happening here will go from country to country. You have once more rocked the cradle of reputation. The fame of O'Casey is born tonight."[5] And in spite of what Austin Clarke and others have said about Yeats' jealousy of Fitzmaurice, Yeats defended the Kerry dramatist just as he defended Synge and O'Casey. In a letter written in the 1930s to students in California, Yeats praised the peasant dialects of the west of Ireland as powerful instruments of literature. Though tempermentally he could not possibly have liked Fitzmaurice's antiheroic vision of things, he went on to say that "the dialect drama in the hands of Mr. Fitzmaurice ... took a new turn,"[6] meaning, he said, that

Fitzmaurice's wonderful dialogue was full of extravagant images and that it was close to the reality of an older culture. What Yeats did not say was that the very authenticity of Fitzmaurice's dialogue, its rhythm and poetic imagery, necessitates his plays being acted by Irish men and women. It is probable that this very dialect—so close to the Gaelic—necessitates native Irish actors and thus discourages production outside Ireland.

At the time of his death in 1963 Fitzmaurice was virtually unknown. Since then his reputation has grown. Recent productions by the Abbey Theatre Company of *The Ointment Blue, The Magic Glasses,* and *The Dandy Dolls* have revived interest of Dublin audiences in his neglected plays. Playgoers respond to the exuberance of his fantasy. Scholarly interest in Fitzmaurice has been sparked as well. This book is the third about his work in as many years. The ultimate question to be asked about any author, though, is not how much interest there is in his work, but rather what makes his work good.

What makes Fitzmaurice's plays good is that they deal not only with external reality, that is, with a concrete reconstruction of peasant life in plays like *The Country Dressmaker,* but also, and much more interestingly, in his fantasies, with internal reality— the fears, dreams, even the hallucinations of the folk mind. Bryan MacMahon, another Kerry dramatist, tells a story which illustrates the recognition most people make of this coexistence of external and internal reality in Fitzmaurice's work.

Many years ago an old rabbit-trapper said to me: "I was ferretin' in Duagh when the duck lid up on me." "Bad luck to you," says I with my ear to the burrow, "you'll keep me here till morning."
    I heard a voice comin' from under the ground. It was tellin' of kings and queens, of moonlighters, quack doctors, of pookas [fairies] and chariots ridin' the night sky.
"I'm bewitched," I told myself. I peeped through the bushes an' I seen Parson Fitzmaurice's son George struttin' up and down the field and he manufacturin' drama.[7]

Many playwrights have fashioned wild and extravagant folktales into well constructed conventional plays, but Fitzmaurice's fantasies are not conventional, well-made plays. Fitzmaurice's unique contribution is his innovation and discovery in form and technique. When Fitzmaurice started writing plays,

Irish drama hardly existed; all the more amazing, then, that he experimented with dramatic form. Though many, most notably Joseph Holloway, say that Fitzmaurice was merely a poor imitator of Synge, his work is not like Synge's at all. His best plays, his fantasies, embody folk imagination at the same time that they exhibit technical creativity: though they are fashioned like folktales, they succeed as drama. He has combined the narrative and dramatic forms in a way that has never been tried before, and in so doing, he deserves to be named Ireland's most adventurous folk dramatist. This study, then marks a long overdue tribute to one of the most innovative writers to come out of the Irish Literary Renaissance.

Notes and References

Chapter One

1. Letter to John Quinn, October 4, 1907; in Allan Wade, ed., *The Letters of W. B. Yeats* (London, 1954), pp. 495, 496.
2. Letter to Florence Farr, October 7, 1907, in ibid., p. 499.
3. Robert Hogan and Michael J. O'Neill, ed *Joseph Halloway's Abbey Theatre: A Selection from His Unpublished Journal: Impressions of a Dublin Playgoer* (Carbondale, 1967), p. 94.
4. Mrs. Marjorie Fitzmaurice, widow of Colonel Wilfred Fitzmaurice, in a letter to the author in 1971 wrote: "The Reverend George Fitzmaurice died when his family was still young and his family moved to a farm, called Kilcarabeg, where a boy who had been employed at Bedford House, helped them run the farm. From this time they saw more and more of their mother's relations and less of their father's, but they remained members of their father's church."
5. From an interview between Nora Kelley and Bryan MacMahon, another Kerry playwright, in August, 1970, at Ballybunion, a seacoast town near Listowel. Quoted in Nora Kelley's "George Fitzmaurice, 1877–1903: A Biographical and Critical Study" (Ph.D. diss. New York University, 1973).
6. Quoted from Marjorie Fitzmaurice letter to author, June 24, 1971.
7. Austin Clarke, ed., *The Plays of George Fitzmaurice: Dramatic Fantasies* (Dublin, 1967), p. x; hereafter cited as *Dramatic Fantasies.*
8. Howard K. Slaughter, "A Biographical Study of Irish Dramatist George Fitzmaurice, Together With Critical Editions of His Folk and Realistic Plays" (Ph.D. diss., Univeristy of Pittsburgh, 1966), p. 41.
9. Kelley, "George Fitzmaurice," p. 84.
10. It is not clear why Fitzmaurice recorded fourteen when he actually wrote seventeen plays.
11. Slaughter, "A Biographical Study," p. 42.
12. Irving Wardle, "George Fitzmaurice," *The London Magazine,* February 1965, p. 69.
13. Ann Saddlemyer, "Worn Out With Dreams," in *The World of W. B. Yeats,* ed. Robin Skelton and Ann Saddlemyer (Seattle, 1965), p. 75.
14. Ibid., p. 82.

Chapter Two

1. William Smith Clark, *The Early Irish Stage: The Beginnings to 1720* (New York, 1955), p. 2

2. Charles Parnell was elected to the English Parliament in 1875. In 1880 he became president of the Land League and it was mostly through his work that the Gladstone government finally passed the Land Act in 1881 which recognized that tenants had certain rights. Irish hopes for Home Rule now focused on Parnell. In 1889 a Captain O'Shea sued for divorce from his wife Kitty, naming Parnell corespondent. This was the end of Parnell's political career and of immediate hopes for Home Rule.

3. In 1856 Ernest Renan explored Brittany and in *The Poetry of the Celtic Races* claimed to have discovered the Celt. In 1866 Matthew Arnold in *The Cornhill Magazine* elaborated Renan's description of the Celtic movement in literature and advocated a Chair of Celtic Languages at Oxford. John Rhys in 1882 published *Celtic Britain* and published *The Origin and Growth of Religion as Illustrated by Celtic Heathendom*. At the same time in France Henri d'Arbois de Jubainville published *Le Cycle Mythologique irlandais et al mythologie celtique* and Anatole Le Braz published *Le Théâtre Celtique*. By the beginning of the twentieth century scholars, organizations, and editors of journals devoted themselves to the recovery of the Celt. The greatest "Celtic" impulse came from Ireland. Many people, including Ibsen, claimed a Celtic heritage. The Celts are found in Ireland, Wales, Scotland, and Brittany. If one has difficulty understanding precisely what this "Celtic" phenomenon is all about, he or she can take heart from Lady Gregory's statement that "I myself never quite understood the meaning of the 'Celtic movement,' which we were said to belong to" (Lady Augusta Gregory, *Our Irish Theatre* [New York, 1913], p. 9).

4. William Butler Yeats, "The Message of the Folklorist," *The Speaker*, August 19, 1893, pp. 188–89.

5. Lady Gregory, *Our Irish Theatre*, pp. 6, 7.

6. Ibid., p. 8, 9.

7. Edward Martyn, novelist and playwright, was a neighbor of Lady Gregory's. In 1902 he quarreled with Yeats over the direction in which the Irish Literary Theatre was moving. He abandoned the theater and playwrighting for the next ten years. In 1912 he began writing plays for the Independent Theater Company, a theater devoted to importing continental drama. Martyn has been called the "Irish Ibsen," so it is not difficult to see why he quarreled with Yeats. Yeats accused Ibsen of superficiality and of lacking beautiful and vivid language.

8. George Moore, novelist and playwright, left Ireland in 1911 to go to England to work on his autobiography *Hail and Farewell* in which he excoriates his Irish associates at the Abbey.

9. Lady Gregory, *Our Irish Theater*, p. 90.

10. Maurice Kennedy. "George Fitzmaurice: Sketch for a Portrait," *Irish Writing*, June, 1951, p. 39.

11. Nora Kelley, "George Fitzmaurice."

12. Quoted in ibid, p. 94.

Chapter Three

1. Alan Wade, ed., *The Letters of W. B. Yeats* (London, 1954), p. 495.

2. W. B. Yeats, ed., *Irish Folk Stories and Fairy Tales*, (New York, n.d.), p. 8.

3. W. B. Yeats, *Plays and Controversies* (London, 1923), p. 146.

4. Bernard Shaw, *Complete Plays With Prefaces* (New York, 1962), II, 517.

5. Austin Clarke, *The Plays of George Fitzmaurice: Dramatic Fantasies* (Dublin, 1967), p. viii.

6. Ibid., p. x.

7. The fairies have three great festivals in the year—May Eve, Midsummer Eve, November Eve. On May Eve they fight for the best grain of the harvest. If anyone should be near, he would merely see a great wind whirling everything into the air as he passed. When the wind makes the straw and leaves whirl, that is the fairies, and the peasantry take off their hats and say, "God bless them."

8. Slaughter, "A Biographical Study," p. 39.

9. Kennedy, "George Fitzmaurice," p. 38.

10. Clarke, *Dramatic Fantasies*, p. viii.

11. Ibid., p. xv.

12. Slaughter, "A Biographical Study," p. 10.

13. Yeats, *Plays and Controversies*, pp. 120, 121.

14. W. B. Yeats, "A Defense of the Abbey Theatre," *The Dublin Magazine*, April–June, 1926, p. 9. This essay consists of a speech delivered at a meeting of the Dublin Literary Society, on February 23.

15. In her dissertation Nora Kelly writes: "It is doubtful that George's father had been an Irish speaker; very few of his class were and Gaelic was not taught at that time in Trinity. After his death, his children became exposed to the culture of their mother's family" (p. 17).

16. Douglas Hyde, *Besides the Fire* (London, 1890).

17. Clarke, *Dramatic Fantasies*, p. 8.

18. Howard K. Slaughter, ed., *The Plays of George Fitzmaurice: Realistic Plays* (Dublin, 1970), pp. 26, 27; hereafter cited as *Realistic plays*.

19. Kennedy, "George Fitzmaurice: Sketch for a Portrait," p. 39.

20. Ernest A. Boyd, *The Contemporary Drama of Ireland* (Boston, 1917), pp. 148, 149.

21. *Choice* June 1968, p. 516.

22. Aurora Gardner Simms, *Library Journal*, February 15, 1968, p. 770.

23. Austin Clarke, "The Dramatic Fantasies of George Fitzmaurice," *The Dublin Magazine*, April-June, 1940, p. 10.

24. Hogan and O'Neill, eds., *Joseph Holloway's Abbey Theater*, p. 94.

25. Yeats. *Plays and Controversies*, pp. 120, 121.

26. Howard K. Slaughter, ed., *The Plays of George Fitzmaurice: Folk Plays*, (Dublin, 1970), p. 129; hereafter cited as *Folk Plays*.

27. Ibid., p. 131.

28. Ibid., p. 143.

29. Ibid., p. 82.

30. Ibid., p. 8.

31. Ibid., p. 71.

32. Ibid., p. 26.

33. Ibid., p. 96.

34. Clarke *Dramatic Fantasies*, p. 15.

35. Slaughter, *Folk Plays*, p. 3.

36. Ibid., p. 82.

37. Lady Augusta Gregory, *Poets and Dreamers* (Dublin, 1903), pp. 128, 129.

38. Tir-na-n-ogue, that is, the country of the Young, for age and death have not found it; neither tears nor loud laughter have gone near it. According to many stories; Tir-na-n-ogue is the favorite dwelling of the fairies. Some say it is the island of the living, the island of victories, and an underwater land. Tir-na-n-ogue is also a terrestrial paradise.

39. Yeats, ed., *Irish Folk Stories and Fairy Tales*, p. xi.

40. Emily Hahn, *Fractured Emerald: Ireland* (Garden City, N.Y., 1971), p. 111.

Chapter Four

1. From the statement of principles of the newly founded Irish Literary Theatre drawn up by Yeats with the help of Lady Gregory, 1898. Quoted in Lady Gregory, *Our Irish Theatre*, pp. 8,9.

2. Ibid., p. 91.

3. J. D. Riley, "The Plays of George Fitzmaurice," *The Dublin Magazine*, January-March, 1955, p. 7.

4. Hogan and O'Neill, eds. *Joseph Holloway's Abbey Theatre*, p. 95.

5. Riley, "The Plays of George Fitzmaurice," pp. 12, 13.

6. Slaughter, "A Biographical Study," p. 36.

7. "The Dramatic Fantasies of George Fitzmaurice," p. 9.

8. Riley, "The Plays of George Fitzmaurice," p. 7.

9. W. B. Yeats, "The Message of the Folklorist," *The Speaker*, August 19, 1893, p. 189.

10. Clarke, *Dramatic Fantasies*, pp. vii-viii.

Chapter Five

1. Hogan and O'Neill, eds., *Joseph Holloway's Abbey Theatre*, pp. 214, 215.
2. Howard Slaughter, *George Fitzmaurice and His Enchanted Land* (Dublin, 1972).
3. Micheal OhAodha, *Theatre in Ireland* (Totowo, N.J., 1974), p. 71.

Chapter Six

1. W. B. Yeats, *The Arrow*, (1906), in *The Collected Works of W. B. Yeats*, (Stratford on Avon, 1908), IV, 226.
2. Lady Gregory, *Our Irish Thatre*, p. 76.
3. Ernest A. Boyd, *Ireland's Literary Renaissance* (New York, 1922), p. 359.
4. Andrew E. Malone, *The Irish Drama* (London, 1929), p. 169.
5. The argument of Alan Price's *Synge and Anglo-Irish Drama* (London, 1961) is that nearly all of Synge's work, namely, his drama and his prose, centers around the theme of the tension between dream and actuality. Certainly whatever ideas I express here about Synge's use of this theme have been formed with Price's work in mind.
6. Slaughter, *Realistic Plays*, p. 3.
7. Ibid., p. 120.
8. Ibid., p. 26.
9. Lady Gregory, *The Wrens, The Image and Other Plays* (London, 1922), p. 252.
10. Elizabeth Coxhead, *J. M. Synge and Lady Gregory* (London, 1962), p. 10.
11. Elizabeth Coxhead, *Lady Gregory: A Literary Portrait* (London, 1961), pp. 41, 42.

Chapter Seven

1. Austin Clarke [obituary], *The Irish Press*, May 22, 1963, p. 8.
2. Howard K. Slaughter, "Fitzmaurice and the Abbey," *The Educational Theatre Journal*, May, 1970, p. 148.
3. Sean McCann, ed., *The Story of the Abbey Theatre* (London, 1967), p. 75.
4. John Conbere, "The Obscurity of George Fitzmaurice," *EIRE-Ireland*, Spring, 1971, pp. 21, 22.
5. Allan Wade, ed., *The Letters of W. B. Yeats* (London, 1954), p. 495, 496.
6. Hogan and O'Neill, eds. *Joseph Holloway's Abbey Theatre*, p. 95.
7. Wade, *Letters*, p. 496.
8. Interestingly, Slaughter writes the following in his "A Biographical Study": "A few years later, Liam Miller produced *The Moonlighter*,

but in order to do so, he had to obtain a release from the Abbey Theatre. Opening night for the Earlsfort Players' production at the Peacock Theatre was Monday, September 13, 1948. The producer wished to do the play in three rather than four acts and found the author one evening in the Winter Garden Palace, a pub on St. Stephen's Green, West, which Fitzmaurice liked because its name suggested a music hall. The playwright readily agreed and that same evening, over a few jars, and a few pipefuls of Bendigo tobacco, made the necessary cuts to combine the first and second scenes into one act. He was a fine theatre craftsman when given the opportunity" (pp. 35–36).

Does this story as reported by Slaughter contradict the story given by Maurice Kennedy that Fitzmaurice would not cut one line of dialogue? Certainly the "readily agreed" undercuts the idea that Fitzmaurice, like Synge, would never cut a line of dialogue.

9. Hogan and O'Neill, eds., *Joseph Holloway's Abbey Theatre*, p. 95.

10. Glen O'Malley and Donald Torchina, eds., "Letters from W. B. Yeats to Lady Gregory," *A Review of English Literature*, July, 1963, p. 5.

11. McCann, ed., *The Story of the Abbey Theatre*, p. 18.

12. Herbert Howarth, *The Irish Writers, 1880–1940* (London, 1958).

13. Sean O'Casey, *Inishfallen, Fare Thee Well* (New York, 1960), p. 169.

14. Ibid., p. 171.

15. Ibid., pp. 246, 247.

16. Ibid., p. 371.

17. In 1928 the Abbey Theatre directors, under the leadership of Yeats, rejected O'Casey's expressionistic play, *The Silver Tassie*. O'Casey was furious because his three previous plays, *The Shadow of a Gunman, Juno and the Paycock,* and *The Plough and the Stars* had saved the financially ailing Abbey from ruin. O'Casey was angry at Yeats for what he saw as Yeats' refusal to take a risk with dramatic innovation. As a result of *The Silver Tassie* controversy, O'Casey emigrated to London.

Chapter Eight

1. Interview between Bryan MacMahon and Nora Kelley in Ballybunion August 29, 1970; quoted in Kelley, "George Fitzmaurice," p. 81.

2. J. W. Cunliffe, *English Literature in the Twentieth Century,* (New York, 1935), p. 109.

3. Saddlemyer, "Worn Out With Dreams," p. 96.

4. Ibid, p. 101.

5. Ibid, p. 102.

6. W. B. Yeats, "Two Lectures on the Irish Theatre," in *Theatre and Nationalism in Twentieth Century Ireland,* ed. Robert O'Driscoll, (Toronto, 1971), pp. 84, 85.

7. Liam Miller, "Fitzmaurice Country," *The Journal of Irish Literature,* May, 1972, pp. 78, 79.

Selected Bibliography

PRIMARY SOURCES

1. Books

Five Plays. London: Maunsel, 1914; Boston: Little, Brown, 1917. Includes *The Country Dressmaker, The Moonlighter, The Pie-Dish, The Magic Glasses, and The Dandy Dolls.* Maunsel also issued the five plays singly in paper covers in 1914. They were subsequently reissued from the same plates but with new covers after Maunsel was bought out by the Talbot Press.

The Country Dressmaker. Dublin: Maunsel and Roberts, 1921.

The Crows of Mephistopheles and Other Stories. Edited by Robert Hogan. Dublin: The Dolmen Press, 1970.

The Plays of George Fitzmaurice: Dramatic Fantasies. Introduction by Austin Clarke. Dublin: Dolmen Press, 1967. Includes *The Magic Glasses, The Dandy Dolls, The Linnaun Shee, The Green Stone, The Enchanted Land,* and *The Waves of the Sea.*

The Plays of George Fitzmaurice: The Folk Plays. Edited by Howard K. Slaughter. Dublin: Dolmen Press, 1970. Includes *The Ointment Blue, The Pie-Dish, The Moonlighter, 'Twixt the Giltinans and the Carmodys,* and *There Are Tragedies and Tragedies.*

The Plays of George Fitzmaurice: The Realistic Plays. Edited by Howard K. Slaughter. Dublin: Dolmen Press, 1970. Includes *The Toothache, The Country Dressmaker, The Terrible Baisht, The Simple Hanrahans, One Evening Gleam,* and *The Coming of Ewn Andzale.*

2. Magazine Publications

"Peter Fagan's Veiled Bride." *The Weekly Freeman,* March 17, 1900.

"Maeve's Grand Lover." *The Irish Weekly Independent and Nation,* November 17, 1900.

"The Plight of Lena's Wooers." *The Weekly Freeman,* December 15, 1900.

"Peter Praisin." *The Irish Weekly Independent,* June 1, 1901.

"The Disappearance of Mrs. Mulreany." *The Weekly Freeman,* November 16, 1901.

"The Bashfulness of Philip Reilly." *The Weekly Freeman,* March 19, 1904.

155

"Cupid and Cornelius." *The Irish Weekly Independent*, May 10, 1906.
"The Street." *The Weekly Freeman*, March 2, 1907.
"The Crows of Mephistopheles." *The Shanachie*, Summer, 1907.
The Linnaun Shee. Dublin Magazine, October, 1924, pp. 194–206.
The Green Stone. Dublin Magazine, January–March, 1926, pp. 33-50.
'Twixt the Giltinans and the Carmodys. Dublin Magazine, January–March, 1943, pp. 11–33.
There Are Tragedies and Tragedies. Dublin Magazine, July–September, 1948, pp. 13–25.
One Evening Gleam, Dublin Magazine. January–March, 1949, pp. 5–21.
The Coming of Ewn Andzale. Dublin Magazine, July–September, 1954, pp. 20–40.
The Terrible Baisht. Dublin Magazine, October–December, 1954, pp. 14–54.
The Enchanted Land. Dublin Magazine, January–March, 1957, pp. 6–35.
The Toothache. The Malahat Review, January, 1967.

SECONDARY SOURCES

BOUCICAULT, DION. *The Dolmen Boucicault.* Edited by David Krause. Dublin: Dolmen Press, 1964. Contains Boucicault's three Irish plays and provides a good introduction to Boucicault.
BOYD, ERNEST A. *Ireland's Literary Renaissance.* New York: Alfred A. Knopf, 1922. Includes two pages on Fitzmaurice, calling him "the legitimate successor of Synge and Colum amongst the serious exponents of the folk play." Boyd's uninspired critique is based on a reading of *Five Plays*.
———. *The Contemporary Drama of Ireland* Boston: Little, Brown, 1917. The dramatic movement is shown to be related not only to the literary revival in Ireland, but also to the general revival of interest in the theater which stirred the later nineteenth century.
BUTLER, ANTHONY. "The Guardians." In *The Story of the Abbey Theatre*, edited by Sean McCann. London: New English Library, 1967. A sarcastic, gossipy, sometimes nasty account of the parts played by Edward Martyn, Lady Gregory, George Moore, the Fays, A E, Miss Horniman, and Yeats, in the launching of the Abbey.
CLARK, WILLIAM SMITH. *The Early Irish Stage: The Beginnings to 1720.* New York: Oxford University Press, 1955, A scholarly history of Irish theater.
CLARKE, AUSTIN. "The Dramatic Fantasies of George Fitzmaurice." *The Dublin Magazine*, April–June, 1940, pp. 9-14. Probably the first

article ever written about George Fitzmaurice and, like all that were to follow, is based on the correct assumption that most people have never heard of George Fitzmaurice; it is therefore a general introduction.

CONBERE, JOHN P. "The Obscurity of George Fitzmaurice." *EIRE-Ireland*, Spring, 1971, pp. 17-26. By citing the differences between Irish and English reviewers of Fitzmaurice's early plays, attempts to answer Austin Clarke's charge that Fitzmaurice was neglected by Yeats because of Yeats' jealousy of a potential rival.

COXHEAD, ELIZABETH. *J. M. Synge and Lady Gregory*. London: Longmans, Green, 1962. Short but good examination of the work of Synge and Lady Gregory.

———. *Lady Gregory: A Literary Portrait*. London: Macmillan, 1961. The first literary biography of Lady Gregory. In the words of the author, an English novelist, "this book does not pretend to be the documented biography that must be written one day," but it is interesting and accurate.

CUNLIFFE, J. W. *English Literature in the Twentieth Century*. New York: Macmillan, 1935. One chapter is devoted to Irish writers.

FITZMAURICE, LORD EDMOND (EARL OF KERRY). *Life of William Earl of Shelburne* 2 vol. London: Macmillan, 1912. Shows that Henry II granted to the Fitzmaurice family 100,000 acres in Kerry "in consideration of their services against the Irish, with the title of Barons of Kerry." The earldom of Kerry was not created until 1723.

GREGORY, LADY AUGUSTA. *Our Irish Theatre*. London: Putnam's, 1913. Lady Gregory's reminiscences of the founding of the Abbey Theatre.

———. *Poets and Dreamers*. Dublin: Hodges and Figgis, 1903. Translations from the Irish of various tales and ballads of western Ireland.

———. *The Comedies of Lady Gregory, Being the First Volume of the Collected Plays*. Edited by Ann Saddlemyer. New York: Oxford University Press, 1970. An edition of the complete comedies.

———. *The Tragedies and Tragic-Comedies of Lady Gregory, Being the Second Volume of the Collected Plays*. Edited by Ann Saddlemyer. New York: Oxford University Press, 1970. An edition of the tragedies and tragicomedies.

———. *The Wrens, The Image and Other Plays*. London: Putnam, 1922. Includes *The Image, Hanrahan's Oath, Shanwalla*, and *The Wrens*.

HAHN, EMILY. *Fractured Emerald: Ireland*. Garden City, N.Y.: Doubleday, 1971. A "popular" history of Ireland.

HENDERSON, JOANNE L. "Checklist of Four Kerry Writers: George Fitzmaurice, Maurice Walsh, Bryan MacMahon, and John B.

158 GEORGE FITZMAURICE

Keane." *Journal of Irish Literature*, May, 1972, pp. 101–19. Contains primary and secondary bibliographies of the four writers.

HOGAN, ROBERT. *After The Irish Renaissance: A Critical History of the Irish Drama Since 'The Plough and the Stars'.* Minneapolis: University of Minnesota Press, 1967. Hogan takes 1926 as his starting point, and surveys the work of those playwrights who stayed to work in Ireland—Paul Vincent Carroll, Michael Molloy, Denis Johnston, Brendan Behan, John B. Keane, and about thirty others. There are accounts of the main theater companies—the Abbey, the Gate, the Belfast Lyric, and the Dublin Lyric. The book is a gold mine of information.

———. "The Genius of George Fitzmaurice." *Drama Survey*, Winter, 1966–1967, pp. 199–212. Basically a reordering of the Fitzmaurice chapter from *After the Irish Renaissance*, with additional biographical material gleaned from Howard K. Slaughter's monograph on Fitzmaurice.

———, and O'NEIL, MICHAEL J., ed. *Joseph Holloway's Abbey Theatre: A Selection from His Unpublished Journal. Impressions of a Dublin Playgoer.* Carbondale: Southern Illinois University Press, 1967. For many years Joseph Holloway kept a diary in the National Library of Ireland in which he recorded not only his reactions to the Abbey plays but also descriptions of leading Dublin figures. The manuscript of the diary runs to some 25 million words on over 100,000 pages! An invaluable book. The introduction is a lively account of this eccentric Dublin architect.

HOWARTH, HERBERT. *The Irish Writers, 1880–1940.* London: Rockliff, 1958. Criticisms and characterizations of the principal writers of the Irish Renaissance.

HYDE, DOUGLAS. *Beside the Fire.* London: D. Nutt, 1890. Translation from the Irish of various tales of western Ireland.

KELLEY, NORA. "George Fitzmaurice, 1877–1963: A Biographical and Critical Study." Ph.D. dissertation, New York University, 1973.

KENNEDY, MAURICE. "Sketch for a Portrait." *Irish Writing*, June 1951, pp. 38–46. Maurice Kennedy, Austin Clarke, Joseph Holloway, and Liam Miller are the only men to write about George Fitzmaurice who actually knew him. Their comments on what kind of man he was are especially valued, because Fitzmaurice was such a recluse. Kennedy's remarks are based on a 1951 interview. Though we are told Fitzmaurice was "as easy to interview as an oyster" the few facts and impressions Kennedy provides are fascinating.

MALONE, ANDREW E. *The Irish Drama.* London: Constable, 1929. Malone thinks very highly of Fitzmaurice and ranks him consistently with Yeats, Synge, Colum, and Lady Gregory. Two hallmarks of Fitzmaurice criticism appear here: the refrain that his neglect resulted in his small output; and exaggeration—here that

The Country Dressmaker "in many respects is the most perfect comedy in the Irish Theatre." He discusses *The Country Dressmaker, The Pie-Dish, The Magic Glasses, The Dandy Dolls, The Moonlighter,* and *'Twixt the Giltinans and the Carmodys.*

McCANN, SEAN, ed. *The Story of the Abbey.* London: New England Library, 1967. A collection of articles.

MILLER, LIAM. "Fitzmaurice Country." *The Journal of Irish Literature* 1 (May, 1972), 77-89. A discussion of Fitzmaurice's Kerry.

O'CASEY, SEAN. *Irishfallen, Fare Thee Well.* New York: Macmillan, 1960. One volume of O'Casey's autobiography, written in the third person.

O HAODHA, MICHAEL. "Fitzmaurice and the Pie Dish." *The Journal of Irish Literature* 1 (May, 1972), 90-94. A short explication of this transitional play.

PRICE, ALAN. *Synge and Anglo-Irish Drama.* (London: Methuen, 1961. One of the best books of Synge criticism.

RILEY, J. D. "The Plays of George Fitzmaurice." *The Dublin Magazine,* January–March, 1955, pp. 5-19. If there is any fault in this stimulating article, it is that too many ideas are treated in a short space. To mention a few, Mr. Riley differentiates peasant and folk drama; he thinks Fitzmaurice created a new dramatic form in recreating the folk tale as drama; and he feels Fitzmaurice alone realized one of the more important aims of the national literary movement in setting upon the stage a part of the living folk imagination.

RYNNE, CATHERINE. "The Playwrights," *The Story of the Abbey Theatre,* edited by Sean McCann, London: New English Library, 1967. Argues that "it is generally agreed that this Kerry writer, who died in 1963, has never received the credit he deserved.... It is surmised that he gave up the theatre because of early discouragement." These two ideas are repeated over and over again whenever Fitzmaurice is discussed. Article also takes up the Austin Clarke allegation about Yeats and Fitzmaurice.

SADDLEMYER, ANN. "Worn Out With Dreams: Dublin's Abbey Theatre." In *The World of W. B. Yeats,* edited by Ann Saddlemyer and Robin Skelton. Seattle: University of Washington Press, 1965. An excellent, sensible synthesis of historical facts about the founding of the Abbey Theatre, far less biased than earlier histories written by the principals involved.

SHAW, BERNARD. *Complete Plays With Prefaces.* Volume 2. New York: Dodd, Mead, 1961. Includes *Back to Methuselah, Saint Joan, John Bull's Other Island, The Dark Lady of the Sonnets,* and *Beauty's Duty.*

SLAUGHTER, HOWARD K. "A Biographical Study of Irish Dramatist George Fitzmaurice, Together With Critical Editions of His Folk and Realistic Plays." Ph.D. dissertation, University of Pittsburgh, 1966. Contains fifty pages of biographical information about Fitzmaurice, followed by an eighteen page critical assessment of what Slaughter calls Fitzmaurice's five folk plays (*The Ointment Blue, The Pie-Dish, The Moonlighter, 'Twixt the Giltinans and the Carmodys,* and *There are Tragedies and Tragedies*), and another eighteen page critical assessment of what he calls the realistic plays (*The Toothache, The Country Dressmaker, The Terrible Baisht, The Simple Hanrahans, One Evening Gleam,* and *The Coming of Ewn Andzale*). The text of all eleven plays is a major part of the dissertation. Surprisingly, there is no statement as to what constitutes the basis of these texts. Finally, there are four very useful appendices: a glossary of 181 Anglo-Irish words used in the plays, a list of 51 place names mentioned in the Kerry plays, a summary of the publications of the plays, and a list of all productions of Fitzmaurice's plays at the Abbey.

———. "Fitzmaurice and the Abbey." *Educational Theatre Journal,* May, 1967, pp. 146–154. Focuses on those plays which have received Abbey productions, namely, *The Country Dressmaker* (1907), *The Pie-Dish* (1908), *The Magigc Glasses* (1913), *'Twixt the Giltinans and the Carmodys* (1923), and *The Dandy Dolls* (1969).

———. *George Fitzmaurice and His Enchanted Land.* Dublin: Dolmen Press, 1972. Covers essentially the same biographical material found in the dissertation.

SYNGE, JOHN. "In Wicklow and West Kerry." Dublin: Maunsel, 1912. An essay of Synge's observations of Wicklow and Kerry.

———. *The Complete Plays.* New York: Vintage Press, 1935. Includes *In the Shadow of the Glen, The Well of the Saints, The Tinker's Wedding, Deirdre of the Sorrows, The Playboy of the Western World,* and *Riders to the Sea.*

———. *The Plays and Poems of J. M. Synge.* Edited by T. R. Henn. London: Methuen, 1963. Contains perceptive criticism of Synge's work.

TORCHIANA, DONALD T. and O' MALLEY, GLENN "Some New Letters of W. B. Yeats to Lady Gregory." *A Review of English Literature* 4 (July 1963), 9–47. Letters not included in the Wade edition.

WADE, ALLAN, ED. *The Letters of W. B. Yeats.* London: Rupert Hart-David, 1954. Valuable, out-of-print edition of the collected letters.

WARDLE, IRVING. "George Fitzmaurice," *The London Magazine,* February, 1965, pp. 68–74. Notable for interesting information about North Kerry. There is some criticism of five plays.

YEATS, W. B. "A Defense of the Abbey Theatre," (a speech delivered at a meeting of the Dublin Literary Society on Feb. 23), *The Dublin Magazine,* April-June, 1926, pp. 8–12.

———, ed. *Irish Folk Stories and Fairy Tales.* (New York: Grosset and Dunlap, n.d. Irish folk tales collected by Yeats.

———. *Plays and Controversies.* London: Macmillan, 1923. Collection of essays and criticisms.

———. *The Arrow* (1906). In *The Collected Works of W. B. Yeats,* vol. 4. Stratford on Avon: Shakespeare Head Press, 1908. A short-lived literary journal edited by Yeats.

———. "The Message of the Folklorist." *The Speaker,* August 19, 1893, pp. 188–192. An essay.

Index